CHICAGO

THEN & NOW

Thunder Bay Press
An imprint of the Baker & Taylor Publishing Group
10350 Barnes Canyon Road, San Diego, CA 92121
www.thunderbaybooks.com

Produced by Salamander Books, an imprint of Anova Books Ltd.
10 Southcombe Street, London W14 0RA, UK

"Then and Now" is a registered trademark of Anova Books Ltd.

ISBN-13: 978-1-60710-746-0
ISBN-10: 1-60710-746-5

The Library of Congress has cataloged the original Thunder Bay
edition as follows:

Maguire, Kathleen, 1968-
  Chicago then & now / Kathleen Maguire and Elizabeth McNulty. --
[2nd ed.].
    p. cm.
  Updated ed. of: Chicago then & now / Elizabeth McNulty.
  ISBN 978-1-60710-580-0 -- ISBN 1-60710-580-2
1. Chicago (Ill.)--Pictorial works. 2. Chicago (Ill.)--History--Pictorial works.
3. Repeat photography--Illinois--Chicago. I. McNulty, Elizabeth, 1971-
II. McNulty, Elizabeth, 1971- Chicago then & now. III. Title. IV. Title:
Chicago then and now.
  F548.37.M37 2012
  977.3'11--dc23
                        2012025204

Printed in China

2 3 4 5 17 16 15 14

Publisher's Acknowledgment
This edition of *Chicago Then and Now* is based on an original version
written by Elizabeth McNulty and photographed by Simon Clay in 2000,
and subsequently updated in 2005 by Tom O'Gorman.

Author's Acknowledgments
Kathleen Maguire would like to thank the staff of the research library at
the Chicago History Museum for their knowledge and assistance. Thanks
also to Nora Frazin for her research assistance and to Karl Mondon for his
sharp eye and excellent photography. And the utmost gratitude to Terry
Sullivan for his unending generosity and vast knowledge of the city.

Picture Credits
The publisher would like to thank the following for kindly supplying
images for the book:

"Then" images:
Joe and Jeanette Archie: pages 64, 66, 68, 70, 72, 90, and 91.
Barnes-Crosby/Chicago Historical Society: pages 12, 14, 28, 39 (middle),
49, 84, 95, and 122.
Chicago Aerial Surveying Company/Chicago Historical Society: page 10.
Chicago Daily News/Chicago Historical Society: pages 116 and 124.
Chicago Historical Society: pages 8, 20, 34, 40, 46, 53, 54, 74, 78, 80, 88
(main), 92, 94, 100, 103, 104, 106, 112, 114, 115, 119 (inset), 128, 134,
141, and 142.
C. R. Childs/Chicago Historical Society: page 110.
Corbis Images: pages 32, 82, 102, 106 (inset), and 113.
Essanay Film Studio Collection/Chicago Historical Society: page 118.
Fourth Presbyterian Church; special thanks to church archivist Bob
Rasmussen and administrator Mary Rhodes: page 76.
Getty Images: pages 42, 43, 58, 99, 117, 125, 130, and 138, 139 (inset).
J. W. Taylor/Chicago Historical Society: page 44.
Kaufmann and Fabry/Chicago Historical Society: pages 30 and 98.
Library of Congress: pages 16, 18, 20, 21, 22, 23, 27, 30 (inset), 31 (inset),
36, 38, 39, 41, 44, 45, 47, 48, 50, 52, 55, 56, 57, 61, 62, 83 (top), 93, 96,
108, 109, 121, 122, 126, 127, 132, 133, 135, 136, 137, and 140.
S. L. Stein Publishing Company/Chicago Historical Society: page 86.

"Now" images:
All "now" photography by Karl Mondon and Anova Image Library,
with the exception of page 11, courtesy of Getty Images, and page 83,
courtesy of Corbis Images.

CHICAGO
THEN & NOW

KATHLEEN MAGUIRE

WITH

ELIZABETH McNULTY

"NOW" PHOTOGRAPHY
BY KARL MONDON

THUNDER BAY
P·R·E·S·S

San Diego, California

Every city develops a certain character, the way it has risen out of its landscape, the lasting marks made by its citizens, the impressions left upon its visitors, a blend of what it was and what it is yet to be. Chicago is a city with a history of world-class builders, writers, entrepreneurs, reformers, philanthropists, and scholars; and it is a city with a history of world-class con artists, rebels, egomaniacs, hucksters, blowhards, and criminals. These were often one and the same—and all of them visionaries.

Chicago is a visionary's city. At his first glimpse in 1673, Pére Jacques Marquette observed, "We have seen nothing like this river we enter as regards its fertility of soil, its prairies and woods." He could not have known the prescience of this remark, much less its aptness as a metaphor for what Chicago would become. Despite rapid urbanization throughout the 1800s, Chicago has remained true to its prairie roots in its architecture, in its green spaces, and in the ethos of its citizens. Indeed, its very motto is "Urbs in horto," or "City in a Garden," and it is abundantly both city and garden.

Marquette's companion, Louis Jolliet, envisioned the very thing that would make Chicago the busiest port city in the country: The Illinois & Michigan Canal, connecting the Chicago and Illinois Rivers, opened a water route between the Great Lakes and the Gulf of Mexico when it was completed in 1848. Chicago profited as a production and distribution center for Union supplies, and continued to expand in size and population after the Civil War. The Great Chicago Fire of 1871 could have burned out the city's momentum. Instead it revealed the true character of Chicagoans, as they undertook a rapid rebuilding effort that included the design and construction of some of the world's most dramatic architecture. Chicago was a hard-working city, one that took risks and embraced change.

This is the Chicago into which Daniel Burnham emerged. Architect of the "White City" and the 1893 World's Columbian Exposition, Burnham's brilliant and ambitious

CHICAGO
THEN & NOW INTRODUCTION

1909 Plan of Chicago was a (mostly) practicable expression of his credo, "Make no little plans, they have no magic to stir men's blood." The plan outlined a bold urban-planning strategy that resulted in some of Chicago's most unique and compelling features, including double-decked Wacker Drive, the "greenbelt" along the lakefront, and, one could argue, today's Millennium Park, as the plan continues to inspire innovation to this day.

To Burnham, a rich cultural element was as vital to a city as an efficient transportation system. One of his contemporaries held a similar passion—Bertha Honoré Palmer, wife of Chicago real estate baron Potter Palmer, and a visionary in her own right. Her patronage of the arts brought attention and prestige to the city's new Art Institute of Chicago, and her bequests enriched a collection that would become one of the most significant in the world. It is likely no coincidence that the arts began to flourish in Chicago in subsequent decades, in artist colonies in Hyde Park and in literary salons on South Michigan Avenue.

Education in the arts was foremost in Jane Addams's vision when she opened Hull House on the West Side in 1889. Art classes for immigrants at Hull House developed into a full-fledged fine arts program, and with the influence of the Arts and Crafts movement offered opportunity for social reform. Immigrant handiwork evolved into instruction in bookbinding and woodworking, putting the power of wage-earning in the hands of immigrant women at a time when the city's labor movement was in full swing.

The labor movement in Chicago pitted vision against vision— the ambitions of the city's businessmen against working-class dreams of opportunity. Certain sites around the city—Pullman District, Haymarket Square—have become synonymous with the movement itself. Chicago's legacy to labor is "May Day," the international workers' holiday that arose in response to the 1886 Haymarket riots.

The legacy left by these visionaries and collectives on the character of Chicago is without measure, and largely intangible.

But there is one Chicago visionary who shaped the city in a very literal way—architect Louis Sullivan, whose touch upon the city is visible from every downtown angle and beyond, and is too vast to enumerate here. His work in many ways symbolizes Chicago itself: the sturdiest of exteriors encasing a delicate interior, one of labyrinthine complexity and startling beauty bordering on excessive, utterly modern and profoundly human.

Perhaps a big city is a place to go for reinvention, to become someone new. But Chicago is the city where people can be the essence of themselves. An untrained architect can set a city on its course to become a model of urban planning. A debutante can establish an enduring legacy of the arts in a city more grimy than it is refined. A young woman schooled for marriage can enact social reforms that change the lives of women and children around the world. A man with a vision can come of age, grow, and suffer, and leave the city permanently changed.

Chicago Then and Now, in its 2012 incarnation, shows a city coming of age, growing, suffering, and embracing change. It shows a city looking forward, facing its share of catastrophes and critics and boldly proceeding. It shows a city that, in its essence, is utterly modern and profoundly human.

Born and raised here, I've lived on each of Chicago's three sides, swum in its lake and sailed on its river, walked its sidewalks and ridden its trains, and answered proudly whenever someone would ask where I'm from. In my life I've watched my city prosper and falter, grow and regress. I've seen it lit with fire and covered with ice, admired it from afar and been swallowed whole from within. It has shaped me. And now I have a chance to honor it, and all that I thought I knew.

Wabash Avenue, 1905   p. 14

Chicago Theatre, 1949   p. 31

Art Institute of Chicago, 1895   p. 38

The Rookery, 1893   p. 45

Dearborn Street Station, 1915   p. 48

Chicago and North Western Terminal, 1911   p. 50

State Street Bridge, 1900   p. 54

Illinois Central Railyards, 1942   p. 62

North Michigan Avenue, 1950   p. 64

Water Tower, 1891   *p. 74*

Lake Shore Drive, 1905   *p. 79*

Chicago River South Branch, 1860   *p. 88*

The Great Chicago Fire, 1871   *p. 102*

Lincoln Park, 1900   *p. 108*

Wrigley Field, 1915   *p. 116*

Union Stock Yards, 1907   *p. 120*

Comiskey Park, 1913   *p. 124*

Museum of Science and Industry, 1893   *p. 134*

1936

CHICAGO FROM THE AIR

The world's largest commercial building has been dwarfed by seventy years of progress

ABOVE: By the 1930s, Chicago was already shaping up as the home of America's boldest architecture. This 1936 view to the north-northeast includes some recently completed gems of the era, such as the thronelike Civic Opera Building (1929) at left along the South Branch of the Chicago River; the hulking Merchandise Mart (1930) on the river's East Branch, with 4.1 million square feet, still the world's largest commercial building today; and, at center, Chicago's most famous Art Deco building, the Chicago Board of Trade (1930), topped with the pyramid.

ABOVE: The muscular Merchandise Mart remains a significant reference point in this aerial view, but is dwarfed by a newer Chicago icon—the 1968 John Hancock Center (far right), designed by prominent Second Chicago school architects Skidmore, Owings & Merrill. Its gently tapered lines and rabbit-ear antennae are instantly recognizable and, of all Chicago architecture, are perhaps most closely identified with the city.

The ash-gray Leo Burnett Building (right center), completed in 1989 and named for its largest tenant, is a postmodern presence in the architecture along the river. Its design includes the steel-and-glass combination of its skyscraper predecessors as well as the "Chicago window" of the First Chicago school, in which projected bay windows form a grid pattern on the building's facade and bring maximum light to the interior.

1929

AERIAL VIEW OF
GRANT PARK

"A noble, logical diagram once recorded
will not die." —*Daniel Burnham*

ABOVE: Part of Daniel Burnham's grand Chicago Plan was
realized downtown in the construction of Grant Park. Seen
here in 1929, the park was built on 220 acres of lakefront
landfill in a formal French style designed by the Olmsted
Brothers. At center is one of Chicago's most cherished
landmarks, Buckingham Fountain. Modeled on the Bassin
de Latone at Versailles but twice the size, the pink marble
fountain was installed in 1927. The Art Institute of Chicago
(1892) faces Michigan Avenue, whose skyscrapers dominate
the skyline. Grant Park is an early example of Burnham's
vision of a greenbelt: miles of lakefront as public space
devoted to cultural enrichment for residents and visitors.

1910

ABOVE: The U.S. Army tournament was held in Grant Park in July 1910, a result of efforts by Chicago's "Sane Fourth" organization, whose goal was to create a Fourth of July celebration free from the dangers of fireworks.

ABOVE: The Willis Tower (formerly the Sears Tower) and the Aon Center (formerly the Amoco Building) anchor the contemporary skyline south of the Chicago River, but along Lake Michigan, Burnham's vision of a greenbelt prevails. The well-ordered symmetry of the Olmsted Brothers' design for Grant Park is a feature of another Burnham ideal, the City Beautiful, in which careful urban planning harmonizes civic and commercial space in America's busy cities. Green spaces designated for art, leisure, and recreation lie symmetrically within urban grid lines. Grant Park is also a site of citizen assembly—for both protest and celebration—including the notorious protests during the 1968 Democratic National Convention and for Barack Obama's election-night rally in 2008. Between April and October, Buckingham Fountain offers hourly water displays and nightly light and music shows. During the summer, visitors to Grant Park also enjoy street festivals, art fairs, and fireworks displays.

CRAVENETTE COATS

1911

THE LOOP AND THE "L"

Chicago's "rusty iron heart"

LEFT: The nickname for downtown, "the Loop," refers to the rough circle of elevated rail (the "L"), completed in 1897, bounded by Wabash, Van Buren, Wells, and Lake Streets, and which Chicago novelist Nelson Algren called the city's "rusty iron heart." The L revolutionized turn-of-the-century commuting, with service to the South Side, and later the West Side, in almost half the time of streetcars. As the Loop became more crowded with vehicle traffic, a major downtown elevated line was rerouted through underground stations. The transit system continued to adapt to population shifts, eventually connecting from the Loop to Chicago's two major airports.

c.1968

ABOVE: Although this station was later removed, several originals, such as the Quincy Street Station, are preserved today. The Rothschild Store with the ornate column in the archival photo was replaced by another building in 1912, and which is now owned by DePaul University. Today's system includes miles of subway, and the L moniker endures as distinctive to Chicago transit.

LEFT: This L veers south to the Dan Ryan Line, which extended service south to Ninety-fifth Street. Tracks ran in the median of the Dan Ryan Expressway and connected to the Loop via the original South Side Elevated. This line eventually merged with the State Street Subway.

c.1905

LEFT: This view north from Monroe Street, circa 1905, shows how the L bisected city streets both horizontally and vertically. The first elevated tracks were constructed over alleys that were city property, thus eliminating the need to obtain individual property owners' consent. Although merchants initially resisted the L, they soon discovered that the trains brought hordes of people into the area as never before, and property values near the L skyrocketed.

2003

ABOVE: Cars and pavement have replaced horse-drawn carts and cobblestones on today's Wabash Avenue, but Wabash has retained its commercial aspect. The Atwater Building and the Haskell and Barker Buildings (center) went up during the construction boom of the 1870s following the Great Chicago Fire, and remain as reminders of typical Loop architecture prior to the skyscraper age, including a new iron facade designed by Louis Sullivan in 1896. A 2007 project restored all the original facades and ornamentation, and included the reconstruction of the cornice and stone engravings. During the project, a previously unknown Sullivan facade was discovered on the Haskell storefront under twenty layers of paint. The restoration won the prestigious Richard H. Driehaus Award from Landmarks Illinois in 2010. Today, the entire block is known as the Sullivan Center.

LEFT: When the block was annexed to the Carson Pirie Scott department store in 1927, the facades were streamlined to fit with the adjacent building (left). On the Atwater Building (center), the ornamental cornice was removed and the stone engraving obscured.

15

LAKE STREET EAST
Chicago's original Main Street

1893

LEFT: Lake Street was Chicago's "Main Street" during the mid-1800s, home to the city's first commercial district. By the 1850s, the intersection at Clark and Lake was the retail center of the city, where shoppers could browse all manner of merchandise, from dry goods to custom-made women's hats. The north side of Lake Street between Clark and LaSalle was a targeted site in the city's project to raise the grade of its streets to install sewers and minimize flooding. In 1857 buildings along this block were lifted by almost five feet and set on temporary supports until workers could fill in the foundations beneath. After the Great Fire of 1871, Lake Street was quickly reconstructed with buildings in the Italianate design, featuring flat rooflines and overhanging cornices, as seen in this 1893 photo. This design prevailed amid the reconstruction of the Loop, being practical for retail businesses with store space below and office space above.

RIGHT: The Lake Street L opened in 1893 with service from the business district to the western edge of the city's limits. By 1896, the Lake Street L was the only line offering service into the center of downtown. In 1973 a North Loop urban renewal project was announced, calling for a revitalization of a fading section of downtown, including moving the Lake Street L underground and constructing grandiose pedestrian walkways and gardens. These plans were never realized, and by the early 1980s, Lake Street had fallen into disrepair. In 1982 the Commission on Chicago Landmarks submitted a proposal to identify a Lake Street Historic District. Meanwhile, a boom in residential development in the Loop brought about a revitalization of the street, helped along by the opening of the State of Illinois Center, which included a facility for both the elevated and subway trains stopping at Clark and Lake, a major downtown transfer point.

RIGHT: Today's Lake Street is just as congested at rush hour as it was in 1893.

CARSON PIRIE SCOTT

A Sullivan masterpiece preserved, but the retail store is gone

ABOVE LEFT: In keeping with Sullivan's Art Nouveau ornamentation of the entrance, elaborate balusters line the interior stairwell.

BELOW LEFT: This detail from the entrance shows the intricacies of Sullivan's cast-iron ornamentation. Although criticized at the time as an awkward contrast to the functional appearance of the building's facade, a recent restoration suggests the city's embrace of its most iconic forms.

LEFT: State and Madison Streets mark the center of Chicago's street numbering system, inaugurated in 1909. From this spot, all addresses have their start. It has often been called "the busiest corner in the world." Louis Sullivan, arguably Chicago's most inventive architect, set his masterpiece and last major commission, the Schlesinger and Mayer department store, here at 1 South State Street. Along State Street, his windows soon became showcases to entice passing pedestrians. The store was soon sold to Carson Pirie Scott and became a mainstay of Chicago retailing. Two further expansions were undertaken with a twelve-story addition by Daniel Burnham in 1906 and an eight-story southern addition by Holabird & Root in 1961.

CARSON, PIRIE, SCOTT & CO.'S BUILDING (Retail).
This beautiful and imposing building houses one of the best known and most rapidly growing dry-goods firms in the city.

ABOVE: Carson Pirie Scott anchored State Street shopping for more than a century, enduring through the economic decline of the street in the late 1970s and 1980s. Designated a National Historic Landmark in 1975, this structure survived the sweep of demolition that had eradicated other Sullivan masterworks from Chicago history. Carson's left its fabled downtown location in 2007, and the block is now commonly referred to as the Sullivan Center. This photo shows the building in the midst of remodeling to house CityTarget, the massive retailer's smaller, urban version of its big-box store. Its merchandise—lower-end "designer" sportswear, essentials for small apartments, and even fresh produce—reflects the Loop's increasing residential population. The Sullivan Center's landmark status affords it certain protections from any major alterations of its facade, so Target signage will not appear on the exterior of the building.

LEFT: This souvenir postcard depicts the now-famous department store in 1907.

c.1908

MARSHALL FIELD'S / MACY'S

The store that gave the lady what she wanted

ABOVE: For more than 150 years, no Chicago business was so closely identified with the character and glamour of Chicago life than Marshall Field and Company. For Chicagoans, Marshall Field invented the department store. He had one goal: "Give the lady what she wants." The enterprising retail magnate moved his business from its original location on Lake Street to State Street in the early 1860s. Even the Great Fire of 1871 could not keep Chicago's favorite department store down. Marshall Field's would eventually command the streetscape on State Street between Washington and Randolph, occupying all of Wabash Avenue in a series of refined granite structures designed by Daniel Burnham between 1892 and 1907.

c.1908

ABOVE: This entrance detail not only exemplifies Burnham's neoclassical style but also suggests the royal treatment customers could expect from Field's.

MARSHALL FIELD

From humble beginnings as a clerk in a dry-goods store, Marshall Field rose to the pinnacle of merchandising success, owning and operating a retail business with annual sales of $68 million at the time of his death in 1906. Field's insistence on impeccable customer service was a refreshing departure from many of the shady merchandising practices of his day. Marshall Field & Company was a "one-price" store, where quality merchandise was honestly displayed with its price clearly marked. Unlike his competitors who stocked their stores with merchandise that was in demand, Field kept his prices low by purchasing stock for the store at wholesale in anticipation of demand. These strategies worked. As Field's partners became millionaires, he would buy them out and bring in fresh, young talent to manage the business. Although Marshall Field had little direct involvement with Chicago philanthropy, his financial support of the 1893 World's Columbian Exposition in Chicago led to the construction of the Field Museum of Natural History on Chicago's lakefront.

ABOVE: Boasting an interior dome bejeweled with mosaics by artist Louis Comfort Tiffany, the store featured more than seventy-three acres of merchandise in 450 departments. Sadly, the Loop's grandest enterprise ceased to be in September 2006. Having been purchased by the parent company of Macy's, the name and label of Marshall Field & Company no longer exists. The black Macy's awnings have replaced the classic Field green, but the large bronze plaques with the store's original name can still be found on the four corners of the building—all that remains of the grand dame of State Street.

c.1905

STATE STREET
Main Street, Chicago

LEFT: Until the 1860s, State Street was a cramped, muddy path lined with increasingly derelict balloon-frame shacks. Then successful retailer and would-be hotelier Potter Palmer invested in some land. Within a few years the street was widened and paved (with wooden blocks at least), and Marshall Field had taken up residence. This photo, looking north on State Street from Adams Street around 1905, shows the popular Gunther's candy factory. A former Confederate soldier, Charles F. Gunther's Civil War artifacts went to the Chicago Historical Society on his death in 1920, bringing the society national attention.

RIGHT: This view looks north on State Street from Madison Street around 1890. Post-fire buildings downtown typically had storefronts at street level and offices on upper floors.

RIGHT: Chicago is enjoying an unheralded success in urban transition, in which former commercial buildings have been repurposed for domestic use. In addition, residential construction has transformed the character of what was once almost exclusively a commercial area of the city. Nothing demonstrates this more powerfully than Randolph Street, the very heart of commercial enterprise. East along Randolph Street from State Street to Lake Michigan, condominiums line the thoroughfare that borders Millennium Park and the lakefront. On State and Randolph Streets, Macy's department store— formerly Marshall Field's—anchors a square block with rapid change all around it. Rising along the west side of State Street is a square block of new retail and commercial space, including the Chicago offices of CBS Television.

c. 1890

1934

STATE STREET PARADE
Chicago's "Christmas Caravan" has been
a tradition since 1934

ABOVE: State Street had already been established as the city's
center for retail shopping a decade before the Great Chicago
Fire of 1871 destroyed the entire block. Perhaps because State
Street retailers had been riding a wave of success before the fire,
they were able to rebuild quickly—and maybe even stronger
than before. The State Street shopping district continued to
flourish through the 1920s, but was hit by the Great Depression.
In 1934 Walter Gregory, president of the State Street Council,
approached Mayor Edward Kelly about a Christmas parade to
promote sales. The first "Christmas Caravan" was held on
December 7, 1934. Sales among State Street merchants that
Christmas were the highest in seven years.

ABOVE: The end of the parade route, this stretch of State Street between Congress Parkway and Van Buren Street, has changed dramatically over the years, illustrated by the block's most prominent buildings today—the Harold Washington Library Center (foreground) and John Marshall Law School (background). Chicago's first African American mayor, Harold Washington, initiated plans for a new library building at the start of his second term in 1987. Washington wouldn't live to see the winning design, but when the library opened in 1991,

Mayor Richard J. Daley dedicated it as the Harold Washington Library Center. Architects Hammond, Beeby & Babka's design combines significant elements of Chicago's architectural history, such as the ornamented semicircular arches of the First Chicago school and the sculptural roof ornamentation of the Beaux-Arts movement. After a short detour to Michigan Avenue during the 1990s, Chicago's Christmas Caravan—now the McDonald's Thanksgiving Parade—is still a major holiday attraction.

c.1885

PALMER HOUSE

A legendary hotel, three times over

BERTHA PALMER
Bertha Palmer developed a certain business acumen and social finesse as she helped her husband rebuild his fortune. She played an instrumental role in the 1893 World's Columbian Exposition in Chicago. As president of the Board of Lady Managers, Bertha established a strong representation of women at the exposition by directing the presentation of exhibits at the Women's Building on the Midway and throughout the fair. She also put her social talents to work overseas, building connections and promoting interest among the royals in Europe. Her efforts gained the notice of President William McKinley, who appointed her to the Paris committee in 1900. Bertha Palmer is also recognized as a philanthropist. After Potter Palmer died in 1902, Bertha took over the management of his estate, doubling its value before her death in 1918.

LEFT: In 1867 successful businessman Potter Palmer bought three-quarters of a mile of property on State Street, which was on the ramshackle edge of town. Within two years, he had transformed the area, convincing the city council to widen the street, inducing Marshall Field's to relocate from its premier Lake Street location, and replacing the tumbledown shacks at the corner of State and Monroe with the elegant Palmer House Hotel.

ABOVE: The Palmer House seen at left is actually the second hotel. The original, which cost the then-outrageous sum of $300,000 to outfit, opened to great fanfare only thirteen days before the Great Fire of 1871. Potter Palmer rushed to rebuild, and in just a few years the rococo palace seen in the archival photo was completed. It was considered the grandest hotel of the day. Today, the Palmer House Hilton is in its third incarnation, an elegant 1927 building by Holabird & Roche.

RELIANCE BUILDING
The birthplace of the classic
Chicago window

LEFT: The mother of all glass-and-steel
skyscrapers—the Reliance Building by Daniel
Burnham and John Wellborn Root—changed
the course of architecture when it was built in
1890. Located on the southwest corner of State
and Washington Streets, the remarkable use of
large glass panes gave the world the classic
"Chicago window," and the interior steel-frame
construction introduced Chicagoans to modern
design. Narrow piers, mullions, and spandrels
are clad in cream-colored, glazed terra-cotta,
enhanced by a Gothic tracery and a flat cornice.
Thanks to Elisha Otis and his elevator, there
seemed no limits to the heights to which
buildings could rise. Burnham, though, was
devastated when his longtime partner Root
died before the building was finished. In young
Charles Atwood, Burnham found a talented
genius with the ability to bring the project to
completion. This photo shows the building
circa 1900.

RIGHT: Despite decades of misuse and underappreciation alongside State Street's decline, the Reliance Building has been refurbished with painstaking skill and is now the Hotel Burnham. After a $27.5 million restoration in 1999, this architectural masterpiece once again shimmers with fresh elegance. In the interior, ornamental cast-iron framed elevators and stairways continue to showcase the genius of the building's great architects. This transformation brought back one of Chicago's most enduring historical landmarks, now named to honor the man who created it. Only a single pane of the original glass remains in place on the fourteen-story frame. The Hotel Burnham has also helped to jump-start a new prosperity along State Street. The hotel's Atwood Café tips its hat to the young man responsible for completing this revolutionary addition to Chicago's influence on American architectural design.

CHICAGO THEATRE
Chicago's iconic theater marquee

LEFT: Brothers Barney and Abe Balaban and Sam and Morris Katz are responsible for many of the city's most luxurious motion-picture venues. In the early 1920s, they commissioned Cornelius and George Rapp to design the palatial Chicago Theatre. Located on State Street between Lake and Randolph, the Chicago Theatre was the Loop's first movie venue and a model for the design of other motion-picture houses across the country. It seated 3,600, most of whom were well-to-do Chicagoans who appreciated the extravagant interiors at least as much as the motion pictures they came to see. The interior lobby, adorned with the heavy draperies and sparkling chandeliers, might have reminded the theater's first patrons of the French Empire. After paying fifty cents for an evening show, they would ascend the regal staircase modeled after the Paris Opera House into the theater's grand balcony. The Rapps would eventually design another Chicago landmark—the Uptown Theatre. The success of these models was so great that the Rapps went on to become "architects in residence" for the entire Paramount/Publix chain.

RIGHT: This image of the Chicago Theatre's entrance was shot by Stanley Kubrick in 1949 for a photo-essay in *Look* magazine titled "Chicago, City of Contrasts."

RIGHT: The Chicago Theatre's combination Neo-Baroque/Beaux-Arts style made it one of the first such buildings in the nation, and it is the oldest surviving in Chicago. The white terra-cotta triumphal arch behind the marquee opens into a series of lavish, Versailles-inspired spaces, and also reflects the popularity of terra-cotta moldings on building facades in the 1920s. The iconic vertical sign and marquee—which were a later addition to the building—serve as an unofficial emblem of the city. The theater prospered into the 1950s. Over the next thirty years, though, attendance declined, and the Chicago Theatre closed in 1985. However, less than a year later, the theater was not only still standing but had been completely restored, and reopened in 1986 with a headline performance by Frank Sinatra. Today the Chicago Theatre features live concerts rather than the motion pictures that characterized its early success, with a range of performers that includes rock bands, comedians, country singers, and even poetry slams.

1949

c.1910

MAJESTIC THEATRE / BANK OF AMERICA THEATRE
Second only to New York on the national vaudeville circuit

LEFT: The Majestic opened in 1906 with seating for 2,000 and performances six days a week. Rising prosperity corresponded to the growing popularity of vaudeville shows, which might include a dozen separate acts and a mixture of performance types. Comedians, contortionists, ventriloquists, jugglers, magicians, and dancers appealed to an audience that was not only socially diverse but also included women and children. More refined than its predecessors in American entertainment—variety shows and burlesque—vaudeville offered a theater experience with an air of respectability for Americans who were beginning to understand how to enjoy their new wealth. Despite its increasing popularity during the 1910s, competition from motion picture houses and financial losses forced the Majestic to close during the Great Depression.

ABOVE: The building reopened in 1945 as the Sam Shubert Theatre—named for the late brother of the theater's new owners. The Shubert brothers were already successful as owners, managers, and producers in some of Broadway's most important venues. The new Shubert maintained many features of the original Majestic, including the ornate designs of original architects Edmund Krause and Rapp & Rapp—the same Rapp brothers who designed the neo-Baroque Chicago Theatre. Major renovations in 2005 also preserved design elements of the original Majestic, including the lobby's mosaic-tile floor and paint to match its original colors. The theater reopened in May 2006 as the LaSalle Bank Theatre, and was renamed the Bank of America Theatre two years later, after LaSalle Bank's new owner.

1928

OLD CHICAGO
STOCK EXCHANGE
A lost architectural masterpiece

LEFT: Perhaps no single piece of Chicago architecture is more sadly missed than the 1894 Chicago Stock Exchange, designed by Louis Sullivan and Dankmar Adler. Built at the corner of LaSalle and Washington Streets, it was second in significance among U.S. financial markets only to the New York Stock Exchange. Utilizing the technology of a caisson foundation to adapt to Chicago's marshy soil, Adler and Sullivan created an extraordinary design rich in detail. No other building in Chicago history was more of a cause célèbre when it was announced that it would fall to the wrecking ball in 1972. Its loss signifies a less intelligent era of Chicago architectural protection. No one worked more diligently to save the building than architectural photographer Richard Nickel, who, when the demolition began, managed to get inside to photograph the tragedy of its destruction. Sadly, Nickel himself became a casualty of the demolition—he was killed while inside the building. Later artifacts from the structure became treasured relics of the Prairie style. The interior trading room, with Sullivan's gorgeous stenciling and stained glass, is preserved at the Art Institute of Chicago, as is the graceful entrance arch, called by one critic the "Wailing Wall of Chicago's preservation movement."

RIGHT: Sullivan's design included an open stairwell, which offered another element for ornamentation. These cast-iron balusters lined the staircase from the third to the thirteenth floors.

34

RIGHT: The Chicago Stock Exchange remained
in the Sullivan and Adler–designed building only
until shortly after Black Friday in 1929. By 1930
it had relocated. During the hardship of the
Depression, the building remained vacant. Its
subsequent history was a series of failed attempts
to find someone capable of assuming the tax
burden it posed. Today, the corner of LaSalle and
Washington Streets is void of architectural genius
with the absence of the Chicago Stock Exchange.
In its place rises a structure of far more functional
design, a monument to the previous era's blind
eye to historical architecture and its legacy of
true grandeur. Such important, irreplaceable
architecture is more carefully protected today.

1963

LEFT: The Boston architectural firm Shepley, Rutan & Coolidge designed the first Chicago Public Library on Michigan Avenue at Washington. Its facade exhibits Beaux-Arts classicism: Renaissance ornamental detail along rooflines complements more classical elements such as window arches and Ionic columns. Designed for the dual purpose of housing the city's public library collection and as a memorial to the Civil War's Grand Army of the Republic—which owned the land—the building suggests strong public spirit and civic pride, and was financed by Chicagoans with a 1 percent tax levee. Although many private libraries operated in the 1800s, by the 1860s plans for a central public facility were underway. When the Great Fire of 1871 destroyed most private collections, these plans accelerated. Over twenty years in the making, the Chicago

ABOVE: With the relocation of the main branch of the Chicago Public Library to the new Harold Washington Library at State and Congress in 1991, the fate of this extraordinary building was in jeopardy. It was saved from the wrecking ball by Eleanor Daley, the widow of longtime Chicago mayor Richard J. Daley and the mother of the subsequent mayor, Richard M. Daley. The soft-spoken Eleanor Daley became a champion of this building. Through her intervention, an alternative municipal use was found for this shimmering beauty. As the Chicago Cultural Center, it has been renewed as a space for art exhibitions, musical concerts, and the city's Department of Cultural Affairs. Today, the mesmerizing contrast of the Smurfit-Stone Building (also known as the "Diamond Building") just to the north vividly demonstrates the diverse

ART INSTITUTE OF CHICAGO

More than 5,000 years of art under one roof

BELOW: Shepley, Rutan & Coolidge designed the building at Michigan and Adams in 1893 as the location for the Parliament of Religions at the World's Columbian Exposition and, subsequently, as the new permanent home of the Art Institute of Chicago. The solid horizontal lines and tall arches evoke the Richardsonian Romanesque aesthetic, still at play in the late 1890s. Beaux-Arts influences are evident in the embellished rooflines, sculpted ornamentation and bas-relief, and classical elements like the second-floor Corinthian columns. American artist Edward Kemeys exhibited his massive plaster sculptures of wild animals—including two majestic lions—at the World's Fair, and bronze versions of the lions were installed on either side of the entrance in 1894 to guard the new home of what would become a world-renowned art museum.

c.1895

c.1895

ABOVE: The Art Institute's west (front) facade clearly illustrates the tall arches and solid horizontal structure of its Romanesque design.

BELOW: The Art Institute's guardian lions are not identical. The south lion, pictured here in the early 1900s, faces slightly south.

BELOW: The museum's collection of masterpieces is due largely to the generosity of Bertha Honore Palmer, who bequeathed fifty-two paintings to the museum in 1924. A year later, the Helen Birch Bartlett Memorial Collection was donated, including Georges Seurat's *A Sunday Afternoon on the Island of La Grande Jatte*, now one of the most visited works in the museum. In 1913 the museum hosted a controversial exhibition of avant-garde European art, thus beginning what is now one of the world's most comprehensive collections of modern art. The new Modern Wing, designed by architect Renzo Piano and completed in 2009, now houses this vast collection, including many works that were in storage for years. This expansion, the largest in the museum's history, connects the Art Institute to Millennium Park via the Nichols Bridgeway, creating an unbroken artistic flow along Michigan Avenue.

c.1900

c.1890

SOUTH MICHIGAN AVENUE

A microcosm of Chicago's art, architecture,
theater, and literature

ABOVE: South Michigan Avenue circa 1890 had some fine
examples of the prevailing Romanesque style. The 1889
Auditorium Building (left) was a theater-hotel-office complex
that established Dankmar Adler and Louis Sullivan as pioneers
of modern architecture. The eight-story tower on its south face,
rising above the ten-story building, was the highest point in
the city. The Studebaker Building (center), built in 1885 with
abundant windows to light carriage showrooms, was reborn
in 1889 as the Fine Arts Building. At right is the original 1887
Art Institute, by Burnham & Root.

ABOVE: This 1963 photo of interior detail of the Auditorium Building shows Louis Sullivan's elaborate ornamentation, which became a signature element of his style.

BELOW: This interior shot of the Auditorium Building shows the arches of electric bulbs that lit the stage.

ABOVE: Today, Roosevelt University occupies the Auditorium Building, having purchased it in 1946 and converted the hotel and office space into classrooms. The thirty-two-story tower behind it is the newest addition to the campus. It comprises student housing and recreation areas, as well as classroom space, and reflects the growing student population on Chicago's urban campuses. The Auditorium Theater is still operational, and is famous for its superlative acoustics and sight lines. For decades after its completion, the Fine Arts Building was a meeting place for the Little Room, Chicago's most prominent literary society. The building's theater and movie house have since closed, but its original elevators remain to deliver local artists and architects to their skylit studio space. When the new Art Institute opened in 1893, the private Chicago Club purchased the old building. The original structure collapsed during renovations in 1929, but the new Chicago Club structure maintained the original facade (moved to the Van Buren entrance) from the Burnham & Root design.

41

1887

CHICAGO BOARD OF TRADE BUILDING
The oldest and largest futures exchange in the world

LEFT: William W. Boyington, architect of the Chicago Water Tower and Pumping Station, designed the first building for the Chicago Board of Trade in 1885. Its horizontal lines, rounded arches, and hipped roof are in keeping with the Richardsonian Romanesque style so prevalent at the time, but its long vertical lines and pointed spire lend the building a Gothic majesty, perhaps to suggest Chicago's dominant position in the massive grain commodities market. By 1875 the city boasted a grain trade of $200 million and grain futures of $2 billion. The new Chicago Board of Trade Building also boasted many extravagances. Its 320-foot clock tower topped by a nine-foot copper weather vane made it the tallest building in Chicago at the time, and the first to exceed 300 feet. Boyington designed an elaborate great hall lined with stone balusters, opening beneath a stained-glass skylight. The building included four elevators, and was the first commercial building in the city with electric lighting.

RIGHT: This 1927 photo, looking north on LaSalle from Jackson Street, would have been the view for traders on the lower floors of the Board of Trade Building.

RIGHT: Despite all of its superlatives, the first Chicago Board of Trade Building was constructed on caissons on ground that was essentially marsh. It was deemed structurally unsound, and was subsequently demolished. Holabird & Root's 1930 Art Deco design features a copper pyramid roof topped by a thirty-foot statue of Ceres, the Roman goddess of grain. The exterior clock sits between sculpted reliefs of hooded figures bearing bags of grain. At 605 feet, it was the tallest building in the city at the time. Its vertical design is punctuated by setbacks, a common building element among Chicago architects to allow for maximum interior light. As the anchor of Chicago's financial district, the building has been the site of anticapitalism protests since its earliest inception in 1885. Most recently, protesters gathered in front of the building during the 2012 NATO Summit in Chicago. The Chicago Board of Trade is the oldest and largest futures exchange in the world.

c.1888

THE ROOKERY
One of Chicago's architectural gems
that survived the wrecking ball

LEFT: After the Great Fire of 1871, a dilapidated
structure on the corner of LaSalle and Adams
housed a temporary city hall. Whether named
for the pigeons or the roosting politicians, the
building became known as the Rookery. When
Daniel Burnham and John Root were contracted
to design a new structure for the block, the name
stuck. Completed in 1888, the Rookery, with its
Romanesque arches, was considered "a thing of
light" and "the most modern of office buildings."
That same year, Burnham & Root moved its
offices into the Rookery, which became the
planning site for the White City of the 1893
World's Columbian Exposition.

ABOVE: The *Chicago Tribune* described the Rookery's atrium as "an architectural symphony of lacy ironwork, swooping and coiling staircases, and gilded marble columns that intensify the play of natural light." Frank Lloyd Wright's 1905 renovation replaced much of Root's elaborate ornamentation with sleek white marble.

BELOW: Root's original oriel staircase featured intricate terra-cotta and ironwork. Wright encased much of this in white marble and installed a geometric design that included Arabic elements of Root's original ornamentations.

ABOVE: Frank Lloyd Wright was not only the architect of the Rookery's 1905 renovation, he was also one of the building's tenants. So too was Edward C. Waller, his greatest client and mentor, whose company managed the building. Wright refashioned the interior lobby atrium using a style that can only be called a blend of Prairie and Persian. His signature modern style is apparent everywhere, partnered with a luxurious pastiche of Arabic refinements. This is Wright's only downtown Chicago contribution to architectural design, and his revisions were themselves restored in the early 1990s.

OLD COLONY BUILDING

"Hour by hour the caissons reach down to the rock of the earth . . ."

LEFT: By the time Carl Sandburg wrote his poem "Skyscrapers" in 1916, he could have been referring to any number of Chicago skyscrapers whose "caissons reach down to the rock of the earth and hold the building to a turning planet." Designed by Holabird & Roche in 1894, the seventeen-story Old Colony Building on Dearborn Street at Van Buren was one of several Chicago school skyscrapers with gracefully rounded corner bays, designed to maximize desirable corner office space. Behind the Old Colony stands the Manhattan Building by William Le Baron Jenney. Upon completion in 1891, it was the first tall building to use skeleton construction throughout, the first sixteen-story building in the United States, and briefly the world's tallest building.

RIGHT: In 1976 Printer's Row on South Dearborn Street was designated a National Historic Landmark, and included four buildings designed by the First Chicago school: the Old Colony Building (Holabird & Roche), the Manhattan (William Le Baron Jenney), the Fisher (Burnham & Company), and the Monadnock (Burnham & Root). This block is part of one of Chicago's hottest new residential neighborhoods, and much of the floor space has been converted to condominiums. Over the years, the original cream-colored facade of the Old Colony Building became covered with soot and grime, matching well with the underside of the adjacent L tracks and lending an industrialized flair to the elegant office building. New ownership brought about major renovations in 2009, including a cleaning project to restore the exterior to its original color. Although the results were controversial for some, others viewed the project as one that restored the structure's original grace.

BELOW: This 1964 photograph of the Old Colony Building formed part of a series taken for the Historic American Buildings Survey by Harold Allen.

c.1915

DEARBORN STREET STATION
Printer's Row made use of the station on the doorstep

LEFT: Designed by noted New York architect Cyrus Eidlitz, Dearborn Station (1885) features a twelve-story clock tower and stepped gables along steep rooflines. The building's tall arches and sturdy horizontal design reflect principles of the Richardsonian Romanesque aesthetic, a heavy influence on architects of the First Chicago school of the 1880s. Located at the south margin of the Loop's business district, Dearborn Station became the central point of rail transit for major passenger and freight lines on Chicago's Near South Side, hosting twenty-five railroad lines and as many as 17,000 passengers per day. Already a key site for cross-country rail transit, Chicago was a prime location for large-scale printing due to its lower rates for bulk shipping. As printing companies took residence in large loft buildings on the streets around Dearborn Station, the area became known as Printer's Row. The South Loop was already a notorious vice district, but police raids in the early 1900s cleared out most of the brothels and saloons.

BELOW: Dearborn Street Station was bustling and lively from the time of its opening in 1885. By the 1930s, Santa Fe's Super Chief line was running daily from the station to Los Angeles, carrying Hollywood superstars such as Judy Garland, Clark Gable, and Gloria Swanson.

c.1890

ABOVE: The old Dearborn Street Station has anchored a vast revitalization in a neighborhood that was once crisscrossed with rail lines. The old station has been stretched beyond landmark status and has come back to life with restaurants, bars, boutiques, and art and cultural venues. Acres of new homes stretch for blocks, forming a new urban community created on the railroad right-of-way. Chicago's oldest passenger terminal has survived the upheavals of history, including a 1922 fire that destroyed its original, steep-roofed tower. Its replacement is a Renaissance tower that would be at home in Florence. More than thirty-five years after the closure of the station to rail services, Dearborn Station is as alive as ever. Although the 1922 fire destroyed the building's hipped roof, it is the only rail station in Chicago still standing in its original form.

LEFT: Newly designed downtown rail terminals were beginning to include space for restaurants, retail businesses, and even offices to accommodate the growing number of passengers commuting to work. The Chicago and North Western (C&NW) Terminal on Madison Street between Clinton and Canal replaced the original C&NW Wells Street station in 1911. Bordered by the Chicago River on the south and west, the Wells Street station had limited options for expansion. The 1911 C&NW Terminal, a huge Renaissance Revival structure designed by Chicago architects Charles S. Frost and Alfred H. Granger, included an elaborate three-story waiting room trimmed in bronze and marble, a main dining area, a tearoom, smoking lounges, writing desks, newsstands, and twenty telephone booths. Services available for female travelers included manicures and hairdressing, while men could get their shoes shined or recieve a shave and haircut. The main building was demolished in 1984.

RIGHT: The new building—known variously as the Northwestern Station and the Ogilvie Transportation Center—opened in 1987. Architect Helmut Jahn was already a controversial figure in Chicago architecture. His design for the new terminal at 500 West Madison was in his signature style—forward-looking, high-tech, and cutting-edge. The massive glass-and-steel skyscraper comprised forty stories and nearly 1.5 million square feet of floor space, including a five-story atrium filled with restaurants and retail stores.

ABOVE RIGHT: When this photo was taken in the 1950s, the building—like so many others in Chicago—was coated in a grimy residue of soot from smokestacks and train exhaust.

c.1955

CLARKE HOUSE

Chicago's oldest home

ABOVE: This retouched photo first appeared in a special Chicago issue of *Harper's Weekly*. The Greek Revival style was wildly popular in America in the mid-eighteenth century as a reflection of the country's strength as a republic.

LEFT: A transplant from Utica, New York, Henry B. Clarke made his fortune as director of the Illinois State Bank. In 1836 the Clarkes built a Greek Revival mansion on twenty acres of land along what would become South Michigan Avenue, at the time a dirt path trod by Native Americans. Clarke's wife Caroline described it as "a good home," built with a sturdy timber frame unlike the flimsy "balloon" homes common to the city. Clarke lost his fortune during the Panic of 1837, and the first city directory in 1844 listed him as a farmer. He died during the 1849 cholera epidemic, sadly ironic given that his wife had written to her sister-in-law about Chicago's "good tasting" drinking water. The Clarke children sold the house in 1872, and its new owners had it moved twenty-eight blocks south, where their ill child could breathe "country air." The move required the removal of the front portico, as seen in this 1935 photo.

BELOW: In 1942 the home's second owners offered to sell the historic structure to the City of Chicago, which was not interested. A local church purchased the property, and when it went up for sale again in 1972, the city agreed to purchase what was now a Chicago Historic Landmark. In 1977 the house was moved to its current location within blocks of its first site, facing east as it did originally. Crossing the South Side L tracks was unavoidable, so service was halted and the structure was lifted and carried twenty-seven feet across the tracks on temporary rails. Operated now as the Clarke House Museum, the portico has been restored, and renovations have been ongoing to restore the decor as Caroline Clarke would have done. Meticulous research—including the removal of twenty-seven layers of paint—allowed the interior to be restored to its original bold color scheme and interior design. Today the Clarke House is considered Chicago's oldest home, now in its third—and likely final—location.

c.1900

STATE STREET BRIDGE
An evolution in movable bridge design

ABOVE: As early as 1834, the need for movable bridges across the Chicago River was evident. Major shipping interests relied on the river to accommodate large cargo freights with minimal delays. The first State Street Bridge was of the swing variety. In 1898 a rolling-lift bridge—an early bascule or "seesaw" bridge—was installed at State Street, using an improved design that lifted opposite leaves of the bridge on curved runners. The problem with this design was that massive engines were required to lift bridge leaves, which were unstable in their vertical position. It would be more than fifty years before State Street was treated to the design that brought fame to Chicago bridge engineers: the trunnion bascule.

c.1905

BELOW: A large freighter passes beneath State Street's rolling-lift bridge in the early 1900s.

ABOVE: The concept of the trunnion bascule bridge—known worldwide as the "Chicago-style" bridge—is similar to the rolling-lift design, but the major improvement is the use of massive underground weights as precise counterbalances to the weight of the bridge leaves. The 1949 State Street Bridge accommodates six lanes of vehicle traffic and two pedestrian walkways. This photo shows a progression of architectural forms, starting with Bertrand Goldberg's Marina City (left), a 1967 mixed-use construction comprising two scallop-edged sixty-five-floor concrete towers plus a ground-level auditorium now occupied by Chicago's House of Blues. Just east of the river rises Mies van der Rohe's IBM Building (center right), completed in 1971 as the architect's final American work. Trump Tower, completed in 2009, is a glimmering 1,131-foot signal of the contemporary age with hints of Chicago's architectural history in its Art Deco setbacks and its steel-and-glass construction. It is the second-tallest building in Chicago today.

1909

WEST SIDE ELEVATED

Chicago's "lost bridge" between Jackson and Van Buren Streets

ABOVE: The weight of the bridge halves and the heavy machinery involved in lifting them made these types of bridges unstable when they were opened, as well as dangerous for anyone nearby.

LEFT: Civil engineer William Scherzer designed a bridge for the Metropolitan West Side Elevated Line, or the "Met," in 1895 to deliver trains across the Chicago River between Jackson and Van Buren. Pictured here in 1909, the bridge was actually two separate bridges side by side: one for rail and one for vehicle traffic, and they could be lifted together or separately. This feature was a major improvement over earlier swing bridges, which swung parallel to the river when they opened, halting land traffic of any kind until they swung back into place. The structure of the Scherzer Rolling Lift Bridge is relatively simple; *Engineering World* described its operation in 1905 as "a walking stick with a curved handle lying on the horizontal plane with the handle upward." Weights operated by motors would pull the top of the handle down, raising the long edge of the "walking stick" upward to angles as sharp as ninety degrees. This bridge supported the crossing of 1,200 trains every day.

ABOVE: As many as a dozen Scherzer Rolling Lift Bridges operated across the Chicago River, but only one remains. This type of bridge was an improvement in Chicago bridge construction, but ultimately they were not only unsightly but also unstable during operation. Perhaps it is these flaws that led engineers to identify the trunnion bascule bridge as the type best suited to the city's unique bridge needs. One of the earliest bascule bridges was constructed at Jackson Street in 1915. As early as 1913, the War Department began calling for alterations to the Van Buren structure to improve clearance widths, but the new Van Buren Street Bridge—which was actually on Van Buren Street and not between streets like the first version—was not completed until 1956. The massive Beaux-Arts Chicago Post Office (background) was completed in 1932, but has been vacant since 1995. In 2011 its current owner, a wealthy British real-estate developer, unveiled extravagant plans to transform the building and its surrounding area into Chicago's newest "urban mecca."

1929

LEFT: Until 1920, Michigan Avenue stopped at the river. The north bank bordered on scruffy landfill; the roads were unpaved and lined with soap factories, breweries, and other industry. When this landmark Chicago-style bridge opened, it led the way for the development of humble Pine Street, the extension of Michigan Avenue north of the river. The bridge has two levels, which are actually two separate bridges that can be lifted independently. In 1929, the time of this photo, the first section of double-deckered Wacker Drive was completed along the south bank of the Chicago River from Michigan Avenue west to Lake Street.

ABOVE: Today, the Michigan Avenue Bridge is a gateway to the "Magnificent Mile," Chicago's upscale retail shopping district along North Michigan Avenue. It also anchors Chicago's "second waterfront," the Chicago River. A 2009 renovation restored the original ornate bridge railings. The bridge tender's house seen here is the Chicago River Museum, and allows visitors a close-up look at the bridge's mechanics. This bridge is also the only one that the city adorns with flags—typically those of the City of Chicago, the State of Illinois, and the United States. However, as can be seen in this photo from May 2012, blue NATO flags were added to signify the 2012 summit in Chicago.

WACKER DRIVE
The first double-decker boulevard

LEFT: The idea for Wacker Drive originated in Daniel Burnham's 1909 Plan of Chicago, which called for a two-level street to manage the heavy volume of downtown traffic: a lower level for commercial and service vehicles and an upper level for regular street traffic. In 1917 the Chicago Plan Commission, led by Charles Wacker, proposed the conversion of South Water Street, which ran along the east bank of the Chicago River, into a double-level expressway. Wacker Drive, the world's first double-decker boulevard, was designed by Edward Bennett and painstakingly constructed block by block over the course of nine years. Opening day in 1926 featured souvenirs and a parade with floats representing the various trades that participated in the building of this remarkable feat of engineering. The corner at Wabash Avenue and Wacker Drive, seen here, is often part of the city's parade routes.

RIGHT: The South Water Street Market was a vital transportation and distribution location for wholesale produce, but by the 1890s, around the time of this photo, the volume of goods and the diffusion of businesses beyond downtown made the location less viable.

RIGHT: This section of Wacker Drive along the
Chicago River (looking toward Michigan Avenue)
was the site of the first official settlement here
in 1803—the stockade fortress of Old Fort
Dearborn. It was America's westernmost outpost
at the time. Today the London Guarantee Trust
(1923), the granite building at right, occupies the
same land the fort once did. The shimmering
white glaze of the Wrigley Building (1924) to
the left, with its famous clock tower, sits on what
was once the farm of Chicago's first settler, Jean
Baptiste Pointe du Sable, in the late 1700s. The
Gothic tower of the Tribune Building (1925),
across the street on Michigan Avenue, has the
city's tallest flying buttresses. The Michigan
Avenue bridge tenders' houses are visible in the
background (bottom right).

c.1890

1942

ILLINOIS CENTRAL
RAILYARDS

Soon to be the site of a major city
development project

ABOVE: The Illinois Central Railroad (IC) originated out of the
state's efforts to encourage development beyond urban areas by
promoting its agricultural and residential offerings. Funded by
foreign investment and covering almost 3 million acres from a
federal land grant, by 1856 the IC connected Chicago to the
northwest corner of Illinois at Galena via the "Old Main," and to
the state's southern tip at Cairo via the "Chicago Branch." This
photograph by Farm Security Administrtion photographer Jack
Delano shows the South Water Street terminal at a time when
the IC was operating at a huge capacity.

ABOVE: By the turn of the century, the Grand Central Depot (later the Randolph Street Station) at Randolph Street and Michigan Avenue was solely a freight terminal, having transferred its passenger lines to a commuter station in the South Loop. During the decades after World War II, the IC underwent a series of diversifications and mergers. The yards just south of the river were sold off to make way for further development. Mies van der Rohe's Illinois Center office complex now shares the site with the Hyatt Regency Chicago. The extension of Wacker Drive to Lake Shore Drive during the 1970s encouraged further tourist and residential development. In 2007 the commuter station at Randolph Street was modernized and renamed Millennium Station.

RIGHT: Guests at the Hyatt can enjoy a view of Chicago's two prominent buildings, the Wrigley Building (left) and the Tribune Tower (right).

c.1950

c. 1950

SOUTH WATER STREET RAIL YARDS
Selling the air rights to rail lines allowed developers to crowd the banks of the Chicago River

LEFT: The building at 333 North Michigan Avenue had the automatic advantage of its address before it was even built in 1928. Designed by Holabird & Root (previously Holabird & Roche), the building's front facade facing Wacker Drive is a good match for any of the other Art Deco skyscrapers constructed in Chicago starting in the late 1920s. It was the first Art Deco design for the firm, although it was the last of the four majestic skyscrapers flanking the Michigan Avenue Bridge to be completed. A comparison with the other three might make its construction date evident: the other three—the Wrigley Building (1921), Tribune Tower (1925), and the London Guarantee Building (1923)—all exhibit obvious Beaux-Arts elements, whereas 333 North Michigan is solid Art Deco.

ABOVE: The City of Chicago passed its first zoning ordinance in 1923, in response to the proliferation of skyscrapers that citizens feared would rob the city of natural light. The setback design of Art Deco skyscrapers results in only a portion of the structure reaching its maximum height, as in the thirty-five-story tower that fronts the building at 333 North Michigan. Architectural history is unclear about whether this type of ordinance was an influence on the design or an outgrowth of it, but in either case the setback design is closely identified with the Art Deco style. Its sculptural ornamentation is solidly Art Deco, with reliefs designed by Fred Torrey adorning the building's western facade at the fifth floor, which represent figures and moments in Chicago history.

c. 1950

LONDON GUARANTEE BUILDING / CRAIN COMMUNICATIONS BUILDING

A building suited to its address

LEFT: The London Guarantee Building at Wacker and North Michigan Avenue is one of the four "pillars" surrounding the Michigan Avenue Bridge. With the construction of the bridge in 1920, this address became prime real estate. Completed in 1923, Alfred Alschuler's design reflects the Beaux-Arts classicism that dominated Chicago's architectural aesthetic during the 1920s. Its curved facade makes evocative use of the V-shaped building site. Corinthian columns at the building's entrance and along its uppermost floors suggest the power and permanence of Chicago's position as a major American city. A cast-bronze relief above the building's entrance honored the site's earlier history, when it was occupied by Fort Dearborn from 1812 to 1857. On the ground floor was the legendary London House, a premier dinner and jazz club, host to legends such as Marian McPartland, Dave Brubeck, and Oscar Peterson. Alschuler would go on to design the KAM Isaiah Israel Temple in Hyde Park as a new home to the oldest Jewish congregation in the Midwest.

RIGHT: Designated a Chicago Landmark in 1996, the building at 360 North Michigan still stands as regal as it ever was, though the famed London Club is now a Corner Bakery restaurant. Crain Communications Inc. purchased the building in 2001, adding "Crain Communications Building" to its designations. Ownership of the building by a communications company is in keeping with some of its historic tenants, which include Chicago radio station WLS-AM and the studios of syndicated radio host Paul Harvey. However, in March 2012 Crain Communications relocated its headquarters to the Diamond Building three blocks south at 150 North Michigan Avenue, adding further confusion to the varied nomenclature of Chicago's most prominent architecture. A 2001 restoration of 360 North Michigan included the reinstallation of the bronze plaque of Fort Dearborn, which was being stored at the Chicago Historical Society. In 2002 the project won the Richard H. Driehaus Foundation Preservation Award from the Landmarks Preservation Council of Illinois. In early 2012, plans were reportedly in the works to convert the landmark into a hotel.

c.1950

CHICAGO RIVER LOOKING EAST

The view from the Wrigley Building shows the river flowing *from* the lake

ABOVE: Looking east from Michigan Avenue, this shot of the mouth of the Chicago River shows the locks that enabled the reversal of the flow of the river. By the 1870s, Chicago had become the center of the country's meatpacking industry. After years of providing the stockyards with a place to dispose of chemical waste and animal carcasses, the Chicago River was heavily contaminated, thus raising concerns about public health. In 1889 construction began on the Sanitary and Ship Canal, a twenty-eight-mile channel that included a series of locks to permanently reverse the flow of the river. As a result, fresh water from Lake Michigan poured into the river. Also visible in the photo is the Lake Shore Drive Bridge, completed in 1937 as a Works Progress Administration project. On October 5, President Franklin D. Roosevelt dedicated the bridge and delivered his famous quarantine speech there.

ABOVE: The Main Branch of the Chicago River east of Michigan Avenue has undergone massive change over recent decades, particularly in promotion of the city's tourist industry. Skidmore, Owings & Merrill's functional Equitable Building (left) now occupies the site just north of the river, replacing the Blue Cross–Blue Shield Building, the same place where Chicago's first permanent resident, Jean Baptiste Pointe du Sable, built his home in the late 1700s. Other than the Equitable and Mies van der Rohe's Illinois Center office complex across the river (right), the buildings along the riverfront are mostly luxury condos, hotels, and tourist attractions. The Hyatt Regency Chicago (center right), part of the worldwide chain owned by Chicago's Pritzker family, is only one of many luxury hotels nearby that cater to tourists and conventioneers. The rounded corner of the gleaming new 1,200-room Sheraton Hotel on Columbus Drive peeks out from behind the Equitable.

CHICAGO RIVER LOOKING WEST

From ash-gray to glimmer

BELOW: Looking west over the Chicago River Main Branch, the massive Merchandise Mart (upper right) and the forty-one-story LaSalle-Wacker Building across the river stand out as solid representatives of the Art Deco style. Designed by Holabird & Roche, the LaSalle-Wacker rises from an H-shaped base to allow for interior light, while its narrow tower offers multidirectional views of the city. Construction on the State Street Bridge (bottom left) began in 1942, although steel shortages during World War II and work on the State Street subway delayed completion until 1949. Visible above the State Street Bridge is the 1907 swing bridge at Dearborn Street, and above that are the curved trusses of the Clark Street Bridge, completed in 1929.

BELOW. Today one might describe the view looking west over the Chicago River as either enriched or obscured by the Trump Tower, Chicago's newest skyscraper and the second-tallest building in the city. Either way, this structure dominates river architecture and has altered the Chicago skyline in a way that no building has in decades. The contrast between the tower and the building that formerly occupied the site at Wabash on the north bank could not be more dramatic—the former *Chicago Sun-Times* headquarters was a squat metal structure resembling an aircraft carrier, and was demolished in 2005 to make way for the glittering facades of the Trump Tower. The Trump seems to be a better match to the soaring rooflines and shimmering glass and steel that characterizes most of the river's architecture— although it is made of concrete. The building features luxury hotel accommodations and condominiums, and Donald Trump himself owns the penthouse on the eighty-ninth floor—14,000 square feet with a price tag of $28 million.

c.1891

WATER TOWER

A symbol of the city's instinct for survival

1867

LEFT: It wasn't until the 1860s that the city on the shore of Lake Michigan obtained good-quality drinking water. Chicagoans were accustomed to foul, muddy, even fishy water until the construction of the waterworks in 1866, which drew water from two miles out. To provide water pressure, a standpipe was constructed; the 154-foot tower housing it was designed by William Boyington using Joliet limestone in a style that has been called "naive Gothic." On a visit to the city, Oscar Wilde called it something else: "A castellated monstrosity with pepper boxes stuck all over it." The city's improved water system was partly responsible for the numerous independent townships voting for annexation during the late 1800s, which granted access to the city's public services.

ABOVE: The Water Tower is one of the city's best-loved monuments. One of only a handful of structures to survive the Great Fire of 1871, it became a symbol of the city's will to survive. The tower has been obsolete since 1906, but it is meticulously preserved and spotlighted at night. The pumping station contains the city's tourist information center. The tallest building on North Michigan Avenue until 1920, the Water Tower today is dwarfed by one of Chicago's tallest and most famous buildings, the 100-story John Hancock, completed in 1969. The 1976 Water Tower Place is at right. In 1989 a second vertical mall comprising upscale retail and dining was built a few blocks to the north, underscoring the fashionable aura of North Michigan Avenue.

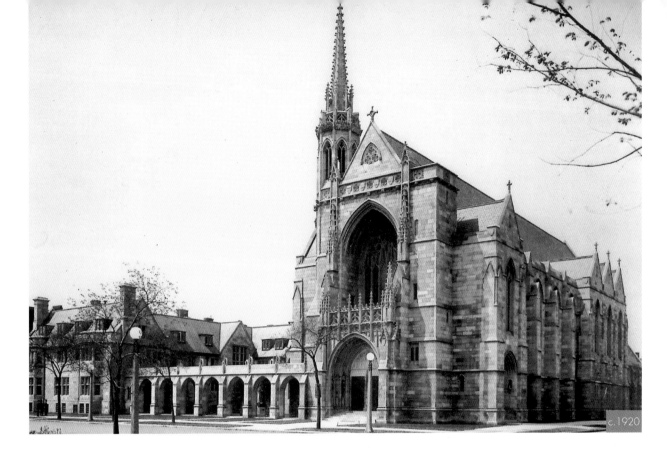

c.1920

FOURTH PRESBYTERIAN
CHURCH
"A social settlement with a spire"

ABOVE: The founders of this congregation inaugurated their first church on October 8, 1871, just hours before the Great Fire raged through the city. The first structure was burned to the ground. In February 1874, the congregation dedicated a new facility on the northwest corner of Rush and Superior Streets. After forty years at this location, the growing congregation and its many "good works" called for a new facility, and hired famed Boston architect Ralph Adams Cram. The Gothic Revival structure, which opened in 1914 at Michigan Avenue and Chestnut, became known as "a social settlement with a spire."

ABOVE: The location at Michigan and Chestnut was a gamble, as North Michigan Avenue was then just an underdeveloped road called Pine Street. It wasn't until the construction of the Michigan Avenue Bridge in 1920 that North Michigan took off. Today, the Fourth Presbyterian Church is the second-oldest surviving structure on Michigan Avenue north of the river, after the familiar Water Tower two blocks to the south. The wealthy congregation is still known today for its "good works," including community outreach to nearby impoverished areas.

1914

LAKE SHORE DRIVE

The grand drive that almost became
Palmer Boulevard

ABOVE: Lake Shore Drive is so much a part of Chicago's
identity that it is difficult to imagine a time when it did not
exist. Nevertheless, Michigan Avenue was the easternmost
street for downtown's lakefront until several changes in the
shoreline, namely the filling of the Grant Park area and
Streeterville in the later 1800s. By 1914, when this view south
from Oak was captured, Daniel Burnham's great Plan of Chicago
had set aside the lakefront for the enjoyment of all citizens, and
Lake Shore Drive connected all twenty-nine miles of it.

ABOVE: At the time of this photo in 1905, Bertha Palmer was already a widow in the Potter mansion on Lake Shore Drive, and the horse-and-carriage traffic would shortly be replaced by automobiles.

BELOW: In the early 1900s, people came to Lake Shore Drive to take a stroll, enjoy the views, or just watch the world go by.

ABOVE: Lake Shore Drive is now fully developed and provides some of the most gorgeous views of the city. In 1884 successful businessman Potter Palmer built an elaborate mansion on the otherwise desolate lakefront, giving an impetus to construction along what would become the inner drive, and in 1893 the Lincoln Park Commission proposed the name of Lake Shore Drive be changed to Palmer Boulevard. Just twenty years later, one commentator wrote, "Along Lake Shore Drive you will find the homes of all the great merchants, the makers of Chicago." Much of Lake Shore Drive, particularly north of the city, is still lined with luxury apartment buildings. The Potter mansion was razed in 1950 to make way for one of these luxury high-rises, designed much more for function than for form.

1922

OAK STREET BEACH
Long a favorite summer hangout for Chicagoans

1922

ABOVE: These women are being arrested at a public bathing beach in 1922. Their bloomers fell short of a strictly enforced regulation length.

LEFT: After 1900, the construction of luxury apartments on Chicago's North Side dramatically increased the area's population. At the same time, miles of lakefront property were being appropriated by the city for use as public bathing beaches. When Lincoln Park Beach opened in 1895 as the city's first public bathing facility, hundreds of working-class young men arrived on opening day and "bathed" naked in the lake. Controversy about proper bathing attire on Chicago's public beaches persisted throughout the early 1900s. The 1913 arrest of Dr. Rosalie Ladova for swimming without a skirt at Jackson Park Beach received international attention. Regulations published in 1919 prohibited white or flesh-colored bathing suits. Men were required to wear knee-length trunks and shirts. Women were no longer required to wear skirts, but their bloomers had to be no shorter than four inches above the knee (same as for men), and tops required one-quarter sleeves. Stockings, however, were optional.

ABOVE: The white sandy strip off Oak Street is Chicago's most fashionable beach today, the place for people to sunbathe, see and be seen, and even sometimes swim. A natural beach, Oak Street still requires imported sand from time to time, due to erosion by the choppy waters of Lake Michigan over the winter. Luxury residential buildings have continued to sprout on Lake Shore Drive, and Oak Street Beach provides a lovely view of the downtown skyline.

NAVY PIER
From Municipal Pier to Pierscape

BELOW: Built on a foundation of more than 20,000 wood pilings, the $4.5 million Municipal Pier opened in 1916. Charles Sumner Frost's 3,000-foot design included ports for freight and passenger vessels, restaurants, a dance hall, and a large auditorium. During its first two decades, facilities on the pier functioned as housing for soldiers, a lockup for draft dodgers, a venue for two "Pageant of Progress" expositions,

1919

and headquarters for the Chicago Federation of Labor's radio station. In 1927 it was renamed Navy Pier as tribute to World War I seamen, and later became an important military training facility during World War II. In 1946 the University of Illinois opened its first Chicago location on the pier. Over 100,000 students attended classes on Navy Pier from 1946 to 1965, when the university moved to its Chicago Circle location.

ABOVE: A *Chicago Daily News* photographer captured this scene of children performing a play on the pier in 1917.

BELOW: At the time of these postcards in 1941, Navy Pier was still a popular recreation site.

BELOW: After decades of little use, the pier underwent a dramatic restoration beginning in 1976. When the work was finished in 1994, Navy Pier's 525 acres included the Grand Ballroom, with its 100-foot domed ceiling; a 148-foot Ferris wheel to commemorate the world's first, which debuted at the 1893 World's Columbian Exposition; and Crystal Gardens, a six-story atrium with fountains, seating areas, and more than seventy full-size palm trees. Performance venues include the outdoor Skyline Stage, Chicago's Shakespeare Theater (modeled after the Globe), and an IMAX movie house. Navy Pier also offers its 9 million annual visitors many restaurants and countless amusements, and a convention center with 170,000 square feet of exhibition space. The former head house is home to the Chicago Children's Museum. Major pier renovations were initiated in 2011, including "Pierscape," an overhaul of Navy Pier's outdoor spaces, which will include redesigned parks and docks, additional landscaping, outdoor fountains, a pool that converts to a skating rink in the winter, and an amphitheater. Renovations are scheduled for completion in 2016.

c.1905

NEWBERRY LIBRARY
Independent research library for the social sciences since 1887

LEFT: Chicago's independent, public, noncirculating library was founded in 1887 with a bequest from one of Chicago's most successful real estate tycoons, Walter Loomis Newberry. Its first librarian was William Frederick Poole, who instituted the collection of rare books and other archives, and worked closely with architect Henry Ives Cobb to design the building that would become the library's home. The Newberry Library at 60 West Walton Street opened in 1905, a remarkable Romanesque Revival structure with a facade inspired by the twelfth-century church of Saint Giles-du-Gard in southern France. Cobb went on to design the Chicago Historical Society's building on North Dearborn in 1892 and the Chicago Varnish Company's building.

ABOVE: The Newberry Library stands as one of the world's great centers of research in the humanities. It has more than twenty-one miles of books on its shelves. Famed Chicago architect Harry Wesse restored the nineteenth-century character of the interior in 1983 and built a ten-story addition on the northwest end of the building, providing additional storage space for its 1.5 million books, 5 million manuscripts, and 300,000 maps in a state-of-the-art temperature-controlled environment. Exterior cleaning in the 1990s brought back the original pink-tinged hue of the heavy stone blocks. The unique material is studded with natural mica chips that catch the rays of the sun and sparkle in a lustrous and shimmering spectacle.

LEFT: By the 1880s, Chicago was the biggest shipping port in the country. Every day, hundreds of lumber schooners passed through harbors on the river, all controlled by the harbormaster. The river was Chicago's industrial lifeblood, jam-packed with freight-hauling vessels and lined with docks, warehouses, and factories. Land traffic was often delayed while ships passed through open bridges. Dearborn Street was the site of Chicago's first movable bridge, a drawbridge installed in 1834 with such a narrow passage for ships that it was deemed unsafe and removed in 1839. The swing bridge shown in this early 1890s photo (in the background at left) had been dismantled from Wells Street to be installed at Dearborn Street in 1888.

ABOVE: Skyscrapers now run along both sides of the river, and its banks load passengers onto cruise ships rather than merchandise onto freighters. Cars have replaced wagons on the bridges, but Carl Sandburg's "all day feet and wheels" is still an apt description. One difference between the photos is not visible here: the underground canal and grade change that reversed the flow of the river in 1900 in order to improve water quality. The south bank (left) is now the Chicago Riverwalk, a public walkway from the lakefront to State Street with seating areas and restaurants. In 2009 the city began planning a massive expansion of the Riverwalk along the entire Main Branch.

c.1860

CHICAGO RIVER
SOUTH BRANCH

"On the bridges, on the bridges . . . always the bridges" —*Sherwood Anderson*

ABOVE: The Lake, Randolph, and Madison Street Bridges peek out of the hazy early morning light in the 1860s, the height of Chicago's swing-bridge era. Commercial buildings and wharves lined all shores of the river, including the South Branch, which led to the Illinois and Michigan Canal (the link to the Mississippi River). Traffic was bad when bridges were raised. Noted one 1850s commentator: "A row of vehicles and impatience frequently accumulates that is quite terrific. I have seen a closely-packed column a quarter of a mile in length, every individual driver looking as if he thought he could have turned the bridge sixteen times, while he had been waiting . . ." On the morning of July 24, 1915, more than 2,500 people boarded the *Eastland*, which was docked at the nearby Clark Street Bridge. The *Eastland* hadn't moved more than four feet from the dock when it capsized in the Chicago River, turning completely on its side within two minutes. In the worst disaster in Chicago history, more than 800 people lost their lives.

ABOVE: Today, Chicago boasts forty-eight movable bridges, more than any city in the world. Eighteen are downtown, and all can be viewed on a walk along Wacker Drive from Lake Shore Drive to Congress Parkway. This photo of the downtown South Branch shows bridges (from the foreground) at Lake, Randolph, Washington, Madison, Monroe, and Adams Streets. All are double-leaf trunnion bascule bridges—a design that uses balancing counterweights, or bascules, to lift each leaf on a trunnion, an axle built into the riverbank. The bridges lift in sync between two and four times per week.

c.1950

MERCHANDISE MART
Still the largest commercial building in the world

ABOVE: With more than 4 million square feet of floor space, the Merchandise Mart was the largest building in the world at the time of its opening in 1930. It even had its own ZIP code. Designed by the Chicago firm of Graham, Anderson, Probst & White, the building is often interpreted as a blend of three different building motifs: the tall tower of a skyscraper, the ground-level picture windows of a retail department store, and the immensity of a warehouse. Marshall Field & Company built the Merchandise Mart to centralize its national wholesale operation. With the completion of the Illinois and Michigan Canal in 1848, which linked the Great Lakes to the Mississippi through the Chicago River, Chicago became a nucleus for the

c.1950

LEFT: Art Deco glass curtain walls and other simple sculptural elements adorn the front entrance.

ABOVE: The structure remains on the site today, its exterior largely unchanged. Marshall Field & Company had leased a portion of the Merchandise Mart's thousands of unused square footage to the government. These offices were relocated to the Pentagon in Washington, D.C., when it was completed in 1943—replacing the Merchandise Mart as the largest building in the world. Kennedy made it a mission to convert the Merchandise Mart back to its original purpose, tagging it as the largest *commercial* building in the world. Showrooms reopened, and the Merchandise Mart began hosting large conventions and trade shows for retailers from around the country. The Kennedy family owned the building until 1998, when they sold the property to Vornado Realty Trust. The Merchandise Mart still hosts many conventions and trade shows each year, and houses design centers and wholesale showrooms. In 1991 Shops at the Mart opened to the public, a retail mall with a food court, transit station, post office, and other services.

transport of wholesale goods, reaching a volume of $6 billion by 1929. However, steep declines during the Great Depression led Marshall Field & Company to end its wholesale operations completely, selling the Merchandise Mart in 1945 to businessman Joseph P. Kennedy (father of President John F. Kennedy).

c.1895

CHICAGO HISTORICAL SOCIETY

One critic described the building as a "pyramidal pile of brownstone"

ABOVE: The Chicago Historical Society was founded in 1857, but its original building at the northwest corner of Dearborn and Ontario Streets went up in flames in the Great Fire of 1871, along with its entire collection of Chicago artifacts and records. In 1892 the society commissioned Henry Ives Cobb to design a new, fireproof headquarters on the site. Cobb employed a Richardsonian Romanesque style similar to the design of his other "high culture" institution, the Newberry Library. When it opened in 1892, one admiring critic called it a "pyramidal pile of brownstone."

1963

ABOVE: When the Chicago Historical Society moved to its present digs on the edge of Lincoln Park in 1931, "the Castle" became home to everything from a Moose lodge to WPA offices, from the prestigious Institute of Design to recording studios for influential blues and rock-and-roll performers in the 1950s and 1960s. Attorney F. Lee Bailey purchased the building in the 1960s, converting it to a nightclub. When the surrounding River North neighborhood underwent a renaissance in the 1980s, the structure became a gigantic, multilevel dance club called the Excalibur.

ABOVE: The elaborate entryway on the east side of the building is centered between two turrets and topped by a balcony on the second floor. The building quickly garnered the nickname "the Castle" when it opened in 1892. The inscription over the arched doorway remains today, identifying the building's original use.

ST. PATRICK'S CHURCH AND HOLY NAME CATHEDRAL
Roman Catholic spires at opposite corners of downtown

LEFT: This view shows the northwest corner of Adams and Des Plaines around 1880. Constructed between 1852 and 1856, St. Patrick's Roman Catholic Church was designed by Carter & Bauer using Milwaukee common (yellow) brick above a Joliet limestone base. The onion dome at right was meant to symbolize the church in the East, and the spire the Western church.

BELOW: Saved from the path of the Chicago Fire, Old St. Patrick's Church remains Chicago's oldest continuous-use building and a thriving Catholic urban parish. In the 1910s, Chicago artist Thomas O'Shaughnessy designed the rare stained-glass windows encrusted in Irish motifs and festooned the interior with complex designs from the ancient Book of Kells. Old St. Pat's, as it is affectionately known, remains the heart of Chicago's Irish Catholic community.

c.1880

1874

LEFT: The dedication of the new Holy Name Cathedral at State and Superior Streets in 1874, pictured here that same year, drew a crowd of more than 5,000 and featured a parade of eighteen bands and a choir of twenty-five priests. In 1880 the diocese of Chicago was made an archdiocese.

ABOVE: Holy Name Cathedral is a cornerstone of the River North neighborhood, and the archdiocese remains one of the most powerful influences in Chicago, serving over 2.5 million Roman Catholics. Pope John Paul II celebrated mass here in 1979, and both Luciano Pavarotti and the Chicago Symphony Orchestra have performed here. In 1924 Al Capone's rival Dion O'Banion was shot point-blank outside a neighboring flower shop.

1892

HAYMARKET SQUARE

A symbol of Chicago's role in the labor movement

ABOVE: Haymarket Square on Randolph at Des Plaines, pictured here in 1892, was the center of wholesale produce distribution. On May 4, 1886, a bomb went off at a workers' rally in the Haymarket district, killing one policeman instantly. Officers opened fire on the crowd, killing and wounding an uncounted number of people. The ensuing melee lasted only five minutes, but when it was over, eight policemen were dead and sixty were injured. Eight anarchists were sentenced to death. Four were hanged, one committed suicide, and three were later pardoned.

c.1895

ABOVE: The statue at the lower right of the archival photo is a police officer commanding peace "in the name of the people of Illinois." For years after the riot, the statue was repeatedly vandalized, even when moved to alternate sites. Today it resides at the Chicago Police Academy. A new monument went up in 2004 at the site of the wagon that served as a speaking platform on that day in 1886, and has since been undisturbed. Once thick with the storefronts of wholesale grocers, Randolph Street is now lined with chic high-end restaurants, condos, and clubs.

LEFT: Wagon wheels leave trails in the dirt on Randolph Street at Haymarket Square. Roads west of downtown were not a priority in Chicago's slow pace of paving city streets.

HULL HOUSE
A pioneering place for social reform

BELOW: After the Great Fire of 1871, nearly 200,000 displaced Chicagoans relocated to the Near West Side. As wholesale business and manufacturing began moving outside of the Loop, the neighborhood became a place where immigrants could find jobs. By the 1880s, the area was ethnically mixed and crowded. Jane Addams was twenty-nine years old when she arrived in Chicago to live and work with the city's poor immigrant communities. In 1889 Addams and a friend rented the abandoned Hull mansion for sixty dollars a month, and opened their doors to the neighborhood. The first program offered by the Hull House was a kindergarten, which was followed by clubs for boys and girls and special events. Ten years after Jane Addams's arrival, the Hull House had become a gathering place for social reformers, trade unionists, suffragists, and other activists. The completed complex included thirteen buildings.

c.1912

ABOVE: For a five-cent monthly fee, neighborhood boys could join the Hull House Boys' Club, which was meant to keep young men from the lure of the streets. The Boys' Band, shown here in 1927, was extremely popular. Jazz legend Benny Goodman played clarinet in the band in the early 1920s.

BELOW: This 1937 photo shows a group of young boys playing table hockey at the Hull House. Children enjoyed playing in this shady spot on hot summer days.

ABOVE: In 1931 Jane Addams became the first American woman to win the Nobel Peace Prize. The work she began at the Hull House continued long after her death in 1935. Locally, the Hull House and its residents agitated for improvements in sanitation, parks and playgrounds, local libraries, and housing. Ultimately, reformers at the Hull House brought about permanent improvements in issues affecting the country's working class, especially women and children. They lobbied for women's suffrage, mothers' pensions, child labor laws, workplace safety codes, and unemployment and worker's compensation. In the early 1960s, the University of Illinois set its sights on the Near West Side as a location for a new Chicago campus. Hull House supporters fought the decision, but were forced to close in 1963. The university dedicated the original Hull House as a museum, but tore down the rest of the complex. Walter Netsch's modernist design for campus buildings (seen here in the background) reflects the rawness of the urban setting, but has been criticized as cold and unwelcoming.

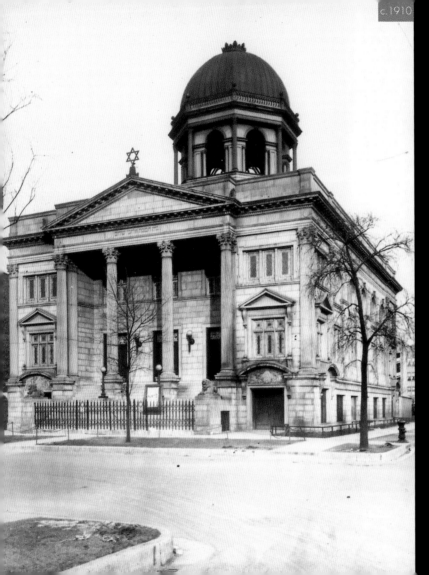

ANSHE SHOLOM SYNAGOGUE / ST. BASIL'S GREEK ORTHODOX CHURCH

A house of worship to fit the neighborhood

LEFT: Chicago is a town of many immigrant communities, particularly on the West Side. When Jane Addams established the Hull House in this neighborhood, she described the ethnic patchwork: "Between Halsted Street and the river live about 10,000 Italians. In the south on Twelfth Street are many Germans, and side streets are given over to Polish and Russian Jews. Still farther south, thin Jewish colonies merge into a huge Bohemian colony." To the northwest were French Canadians, Irish to the north, and beyond them, other "well-to-do English-speaking families." Once families achieved a modicum of success, they often moved on to better-off immigrant communities, leaving their "ghettos" for incoming groups. This 1910s photo shows the Anshe Sholom Synagogue on South Ashland at Polk Street, an area of early settlement for Jewish immigrants from eastern Europe.

RIGHT: As the Jewish population shifted farther to the west, the Anshe Sholom congregation opened another synagogue in North Lawndale, a part of the West Side called "Little Jerusalem." The original Greek Revival–style building, designed by Alexander Levy in 1910, was sold in 1927 to the neighborhood's new—but growing—Greek Orthodox congregation, which converted the synagogue to St. Basil's Greek Orthodox Church. In addition to interior remodeling, the Star of David on the pediment was replaced with a crucifix. However, the portico still bears the original Hebrew inscription. Today, the neighborhood's residents are mostly students at the adjacent University of Illinois Medical Campus, but St. Basil's is still thriving. Sunday services are usually full to capacity with Greek Orthodox congregants from all over the city.

1871

THE GREAT CHICAGO FIRE OF 1871

A catastrophe that proved to be a great spur to the city's growth

ABOVE: The role of Catherine O'Leary's cow in the ensuing inferno may be a myth, even though the origin of the Great Chicago Fire was definitely the O'Learys' barn on the city's Near West Side. The summer of 1871 had been hot and dry, and the whole Midwest was suffering from severe drought. Around 9:00 p.m. on October 9, a spark in the O'Learys' barn turned into raging flames in minutes. As residents waited helplessly for firefighters to arrive, the blaze raged northward, sending off burning embers from its path. As panicked Chicagoans fled north in a bid to stay ahead of the fire, another flying ember

1871

ABOVE: Catherine O'Leary testified that she and her family were asleep when fire erupted here, in their barn at 137 West DeKoven Street. She was legally exonerated, but remains a villain in Chicago folklore.

delivered flames across the Main Branch of the Chicago River, and the fire rushed north and east. These pilings once supported the Rush Street Bridge, which the blaze consumed—along with every bridge on the Main Branch—in its rampage. Visible in the background are the Water Tower and Pumping Station (far right) and what was left of the tower of the St. James Cathedral (center). Chimney remains and hollowed structures like those seen at the far left were on every street the fire touched. Ironically, the house on the O'Leary property was spared.

ABOVE: In less than thirty-six hours, the Great Chicago Fire destroyed almost four square miles of the city and more than 18,000 buildings. At least 300 people lost their lives and a third of the city's population lost their homes. The city's immediate and rapid rebuilding reflected the hardworking and inexorable character of its residents. The Rush Street Bridge was rebuilt in its third incarnation after the fire, but was torn down after the construction of the Michigan Avenue Bridge in 1920, as it was too narrow to handle increases in bridge traffic in the early 1900s. Rush Street north of the river is known today for its famous restaurants and lively nightlife rather than as a shipping route. The north bank at Rush Street provides docking for water taxis and tour boats, accessible from street-level stairways. This lineup of (from left) high-rise condominiums, the Wrigley Building, the Tribune Tower, and the Equitable Building represents a small sample of Chicago's river architecture.

1871

ST. MICHAEL'S CHURCH

"The most impressive remains on the North Side"

LEFT: In 1852, with $750 in funds, Chicago's German immigrant community built a small wooden Catholic church in the center of their North Side neighborhood, then known as North Town. With their remaining $20, they purchased a church bell. It summoned the neighborhood's forty-three families to St. Michael's, named for the patron saint of the church's benefactor, local brewer Michael Diversey. The new structure at 1633 North Cleveland was much grander, built with locally made red sandstone bricks and topped by a 200-foot spire, sixty feet higher than the Water Tower and visible for miles. It was completed in 1869, only to be nearly destroyed two years later by the Great Chicago Fire. Though the fire melted the church's five original bells into one solid mass of bronze that collapsed the roof, St. Michael's was one of only four buildings that remained (mostly) standing in the aftermath. The picturesque remains seen here were declared "the most impressive remains on the North Side."

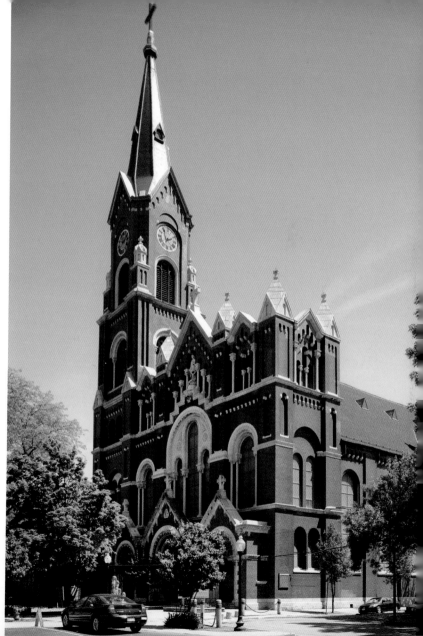

RIGHT: After the Great Fire, determined parishioners rebuilt St. Michael's in just one year. The steeple and clock were added in 1888 and the Munich stained-glass windows in 1902. Today, St. Michael's is the heart and soul of the Old Town neighborhood, whose very boundaries are determined by their relationship to the church. Chicago lore has it that if you hear St. Michael's bells tolling, you are in Old Town. The area came to be known by that name after World War II, when community organizers formed the Old Town Triangle Association to maintain a sense of community in their growing neighborhood. One of the city's most popular events is the annual Old Town Art Fair, run by the Old Town Triangle Association for over sixty years, and named in 2011 as one of the country's top ten art fairs by *AmericanStyle* magazine. The Old Town Art Fair often coincides with St. Michael's annual festival, which is considered the kickoff for Chicago's street-festival season.

BELOW: The population of Old Town today is relatively young, a mix of small families and single professionals who live in apartment buildings like the one across the street from St. Michael's.

BIOGRAPH THEATER
The site of John Dillinger's demise

LEFT: In the midst of extremely hot summers, many Chicagoans opted to go to the movies; theaters enticed filmgoers by advertising that they were "air-cooled." The Biograph at 2433 North Lincoln was one such "refrigerated" theater, and on July 22, 1934, one of Chicago's most famous gangsters, wanted for multiple bank robberies and murder, met his fate there. On his birthday a month earlier, John Dillinger had been declared "Public Enemy Number One" by the FBI. When he exited the show that evening, twenty lawmen were waiting. Betrayed by his girlfriend's landlady, Anna Sage, Dillinger was gunned down as he tried to flee. Onlookers immediately gathered around the body, and women dipped their handkerchiefs in the dead gangster's blood.

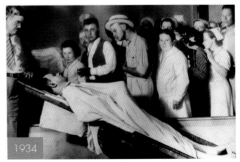

c.1930

1934

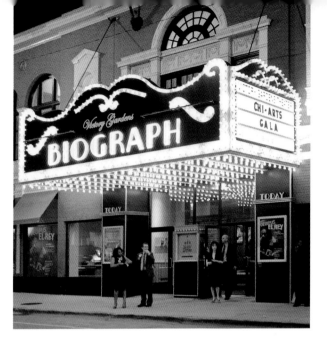

JOHN DILLINGER

After losing his mother when he was three, Dillinger faced a childhood with a strict disciplinarian father. A troubled adolescent, Dillinger was frequently in trouble at school and eventually dropped out. He joined the navy in 1923 but soon deserted. In 1924 he pled guilty to assault and armed robbery, and received a sentence far more severe than his accomplice's. He entered prison a resentful crook, and exited nine years later a hardened ex-con. Over the next year, Dillinger became an antihero of the Great Depression, robbing the banks that had failed their own citizens. The press tended to overlook the killings that often occurred during Dillinger's robberies and to portray the police departments that were unable to catch him (or hold him) as foolish. When Dillinger visited a brothel with his girlfriend in July 1934, madam Anna Sage (Ana Cumpanas) offered information to the FBI in exchange for freedom from deportation.

ABOVE: Today, the ethos of the Dillinger shooting continues to capture the attention of Chicagoans and visitors alike. For decades, when the Biograph was still a movie theater, *Manhattan Melodrama*, the movie showing on the night of Dillinger's shooting, was often replayed. The power of Public Enemy Number One still pervades the narrow alley next door, where the Lady in Red is said to have lured him to federal agents. In 2006 the Biograph was reborn as a new theater for stage productions of the Victory Garden Theater Company, one of Chicago's premier production companies. Its renovation ushered in a new generation of theatrical use, though the historic past of the building will be hard to shake. The building's connection with Dillinger is an indelible piece of Chicago history, likely to captivate visitors for generations to come.

LEFT: After the shooting, Dillinger's body was taken to the Cook County morgue, where authorities allowed the public to view his remains. Over the next twenty-four hours, an estimated 4,000 people visited.

LINCOLN PARK

From a local cemetery to a public park with its own grand conservatory

BELOW: Like the rest of the North Side, this area was considered inaccessible and remote for most of the nineteenth century—remote enough that the lakefront beyond North Avenue was used as the city cemetery. Burials north of North Avenue continued into 1866, a year after Lincoln Park was named for the recently assassinated president. Lake Shore Drive was still a lakefront carriage path, and it would be almost twenty years before the Palmers paved the way for Chicago's elite to dominate the North Side. Still, the Lincoln Park Commission wasted no time in building up the site, and by 1892 the park was already filled with landscaping, walking and bicycle paths, and the Lincoln Park Conservatory (left).

1900

ABOVE: Visitors to the Lincoln Park Zoo view the sea lion's cave in the early twentieth century.

BELOW: Children gather around a water fountain in Lincoln Park in the 1910s.

ABOVE: Lincoln Park is the city's largest park. Its top attraction is the free Lincoln Park Zoo, one of the oldest zoos in the country. Also within the park are the new Peggy Notebart Nature Museum; the Chicago History Museum; monuments to Abraham Lincoln, Ulysses S. Grant, and Alexander Hamilton; a community theater; a city beach and bathhouse; two ponds; a lagoon large enough to accommodate rowing and sculling practice; and, of course, the Lincoln Park Conservatory. The surrounding area is also called Lincoln Park and is today one of the city's most desirable—and expensive—neighborhoods.

c.1895

HALSTED, FULLERTON, AND LINCOLN
Long a high-class neighborhood

ABOVE: Already one of the busier intersections in turn-of-the-century Lincoln Park, the area around Halsted, Fullerton, and Lincoln was home to a high-class residential district throughout the 1930s. Formerly German farmland, the neighborhood has an ethnic heritage that is reflected in the store names. After World War II, however, many homes were converted into apartments, and by the 1950s, the rise of the suburbs meant the blighting of Lincoln Park.

ABOVE: No neighborhood in Chicago has undergone a more refined or redefining restoration than Lincoln Park. The leafy neighborhood enjoys some of the city's highest real-estate price tags. Between the lakefront and Halsted Street, this mile-wide environ is lush with elegance and character. On the western end at Lincoln Avenue, Fullerton Street, and Halsted Street, the Children's Memorial Hospital can be seen in the background. In June 2012, however, the hospital was shut down and replaced by the Lurie Children's Hospital on the Northwestern University Medical Campus downtown, where it joined the prestigious Northwestern Memorial Hospital and Prentice Women's Hospital. Nearby, DePaul University's Lincoln Park campus has exploded into what has been called "America's happiest university campus."

ST. VALENTINE'S DAY MASSACRE

Boosting Chicago's reputation as the "Gangster City"

ABOVE: Chicago's most iconic Prohibition-era gangland slayings took place here in a truck garage at 2122 North Clark Street on February 14, 1929. The event seized the attention of the nation. The bloodbath pitted the forces of Al Capone, the city's undisputed crime boss, against his Irish rival George "Bugs" Moran for control of the city's vast bootlegging empire. Capone's henchmen, disguised as Chicago police, caught the Moran gang off-guard on a cold, snowy winter morning. Seven of Moran's men were executed. The St. Valentine's Day Massacre was immortalized by Hollywood and remains a frozen moment of Chicago's past.

1929

ABOVE: All physical reminders of the infamous garage have long since been wiped away by more sensitive generations of Chicagoans, especially the late mayor Richard J. Daley, who had little patience for the city's Prohibition relics. The garage was torn down in 1967. Thus passed the city's most singular shrine to the bootlegging mayhem of the 1920s. The small grassy lawn of what today is a senior citizen residence is all that remains of that haunted parcel of Chicago real estate. There are, however, many residents and neighbors who, with a long list of eerie sounds and sightings, claim the ghosts of the past still remain.

LEFT: A crowd gathers outside the garage at 2122 North Clark Street as police remove the bodies of Moran's men.

c.1892

ST. STANISLAUS KOSTKA
The original "Polish Downtown"

BELOW: The grandeur of St. Stanislaus Kostka shimmers with renewed vitality and a freshly restored architectural character. Once the gateway for new Polish immigrants in the nineteenth century, today it is the center of a vast urban rebirth. A new population of young urban professionals is discovering the desirability of this community only two miles from downtown. When Chicago was constructing the Northwest Expressway in 1960, St. Stanislaus Kostka Church escaped destruction when Mayor Richard J. Daley permitted the highway to curve around the building. Today, speedy motorists get a jolt when they fly past the windows of the parish rectory, seemingly just inches from the fast lane.

ABOVE: One of America's first Polish churches, St. Stanislaus was founded in 1868. Wealthy Polish beer magnates helped fund the commission of architect Patrick Keeley, who had just finished the Holy Name Cathedral downtown, to design a church in honor of St. Stanislaus Kostka, who was named for the patron saint of Poland. The building, at 1600 North Noble, was constructed between 1876 and 1881 in brick. The towers were added in 1892 under the direction of German architect Adolphus Druiding; this photo was taken around that time.

HOLY TRINITY
Kiev meets the Prairie style

BELOW: The once heavily Russian neighborhood known as "Ukrainian Village" brings together two powerful architectural traditions. Chicago's signature architect Louis Sullivan, father of the Chicago school, blended these potent artistic forms and created Holy Trinity Russian Orthodox Cathedral at 1121 North Leavitt Street, in a neighborhood of onion-domed churches. Modeled on the great St. Vladimir's Cathedral in Kiev, this compact structure, seen here in 1903, is a stunning exposition of the Prairie style. Its stucco plastering of exterior walls and measured scale—replete with Sullivan's trademark decorative metalwork—is a rich and unexpected expression of the style that Sullivan's pupil Frank Lloyd Wright later made famous. Tsar Nicholas II, the last of Russia's Romanov rulers, partially paid for this liturgical outpost of Russian faith and culture.

1903

ABOVE: A century later, the exotic cathedral flexes the artistry of its design even more powerfully, emboldened by a dome of fresh gold leaf. Now enjoying the benefits of a neighborhood with a renewed economic vitality, Holy Trinity Cathedral still echoes with the haunting chants of its ancient liturgical traditions. The interior is a powerful expression of timeless faith, with encrusted icons that cover the doorway. Since the canonization of the Romanov martyrs who perished at the hands of the Bolshevik fanatics of the Russian Revolution of 1917, today the imperial family enjoys a fresh sanctity in a shrine dedicated in their honor. Clouds of incense continue to rise to the glory of God in prayer amid the artistry of Chicago's most remarkable architect.

c.1915

WRIGLEY FIELD
Beloved by the long-suffering fans of the Cubs

ABOVE: One of the oldest ballparks in the country, Wrigley Field was built in 1914 and designed by Zachary Taylor Davis, who also designed the first Comiskey Park. A live bear cub was on hand when the team played its first game. At the time of this photo in 1915, the stadium was called Weegham Park after the Cubs' first owner. It was renamed in 1926 for the team's new owner, William Wrigley. Dedicated to tradition, for years Wrigley was one of the few stadiums with a manually operated scoreboard, and it was the last major-league ballpark to install modern lighting.

BELOW: The front entrance to Wrigley Field in May 1939.

1939

ABOVE: Within the "Friendly Confines" of Wrigley Field, baseball history has often shaped the contours of this great American ballpark. During the 1932 World Series, Babe Ruth hit his famous "called shot" to the bleachers for a home run that just might be the most memorable in baseball. In 1988 the Chicago Cubs were the last team in baseball to begin hosting night games. Wrigley Field is still an old-fashioned park, with a seating capacity of 39,000. The Cubs have not played in a World Series since 1945 and have not won a World Series since 1908. Still, loyal fans continue to fill the seats day and night. In 2012 the Cubs' owners, the Ricketts family, proposed major renovations to the stadium, including additional signage, a large projection screen, more bleacher seating, and a major addition for a hotel and entertainment space.

c.1910

ESSANAY FILM STUDIOS
The studio that made Chicago the home of the Western

ABOVE: From 1907 to 1917, a pioneering movie studio turned Chicago into "Hollywood on the prairie." Essanay Studios (an amalgam of the founders' initials, S and A) at 1345 West Argyle Street boasted the greatest stars of silent films on its roster: Charlie Chaplin, Gloria Swanson, Francis X. Bushman, and "Bronco Billy" Anderson (a cofounder). The studio dominated the market in Westerns and comedies. As Essanay grew more successful during the 1910s, it naturally attracted attention from Chicago's social elite, who offered their homes and surrounding property as sites for filming. The studio's 1915 movie serial *The Crimson Wing* was promoted as a "powerful photo-drama of love and war," which took care to remain neutral and end in a love scene.

LEFT: This 1915 marketing piece promotes *The Crimson Wing*. Gloria Swanson is third from the left.

ABOVE: Changes in the film industry (especially a shift to the mild climes of California), the defection of Charlie Chaplin to a competitor, and internal dissension led to Essanay's collapse. The building now houses St. Augustine's College, a small liberal arts school. The terra-cotta heads of Native American chiefs flanking the entrance were Essanay's trademarks. The building was designated a Chicago Landmark in 1996, and is just blocks from the main strip of Chicago's Uptown, an edgy, diverse neighborhood known for its nightlife, including the legendary jazz club the Green Mill, the 1925 Uptown Theater, and concert venues such as the Riviera and the Aragon Ballroom.

LEFT: The building was designated a Chicago Landmark in 1996. The entranceway still includes most of the original stonework.

c.1907

UNION STOCK YARDS
The facility that made Chicago the meatpacking capital of the world

ABOVE: Located at 850 West Exchange Avenue at Peoria and designed by preeminent city architects Burnham & Root in 1879, the front gate gave a majestic face to the sprawling Union Stock Yards. The facility covered more than 475 acres and was established in 1865, when Chicago was "hog butcher to the world." Tourist guidebooks of the nineteenth century marveled at the scale and efficiency of the operation. Writers had already branded Chicago "the Great Bovine City of the World," thanks to the major role Chicago played in supplying Union troops with beef during the Civil War. Almost a city in itself, the yards included pen space for up to 25,000 cattle, 80,000 hogs, and 25,000 sheep.

c.1909

ABOVE: The publication of Upton Sinclair's *The Jungle* in 1906 led to reforms in sanitation and labor conditions for the yards, but Chicago still dominated the meatpacking industry. After providing employment for the Bridgeport and Back of the Yards communities for over a century, the Union Stock Yards closed in 1971. The gate was designated a Chicago Landmark in 1972. The "bust" over the central limestone arch is thought to be that of "Sherman," a prize-winning steer named after the yards' cofounder, John B. Sherman. Today, industrial parks have filled in some of the vacant space where slaughterhouses once stood.

LEFT: In this photo from the early twentieth century, men walk the fences surveying the stock.

1943

CENTRAL MANFACTURING DISTRICT
America's first planned industrial park

LEFT: Chicago's Central Manufacturing District (CMD) was the first such planned industrial park in the country. The CMD covered roughly 300 acres of land from Thirty-fifth to Thirty-ninth Streets between Morgan Street and Ashland Avenue, close to the South Branch. Frederick Henry Prince, owner of the Chicago Junction Railway, initiated the plan in 1905 as a means of expanding his rail business. The Chicago Junction Railway already served Chicago's stockyards and packinghouses, and was connected with every rail line in Chicago. By 1915 as many as 200 manufacturing firms had located their operations in the CMD. The warehouses pictured here were part of Prince's second industrial park in the city, which ran along the south side of Pershing Road from Western to Damen Avenue.

ABOVE: When Prince began construction on his second industrial development, Pershing Road was still Thirty-ninth Street. The road was renamed for General John J. Pershing near the time of the completion of the first phase of the park, which became known as Pershing Road Development. Loft buildings A–D were constructed in only four months, built in what has been described as an industrial Art Moderne style. Another part of the complex was the Army Quartermaster Depot, two government warehouses used for food packaging and storage during World War II. By then, there were six loft buildings, A–F, which were at full occupancy from 1936 through 1945. The mail-order giant Spiegel Inc. occupies part of the building today.

LEFT: Chicago White Sox owner Charles Comiskey purchased fifteen acres of property at Thirty-fifth and Shields to build a ballpark for his team. Zachary Taylor Davis's 1910 design blended well with the surrounding working-class neighborhood, and included the generous dimensions Comiskey had requested for his "Baseball Palace to the World." Opening in July 1910 as White Sox Park, the stadium seated 32,000 fans. The first night baseball game in Chicago was played at Comiskey Park, as it came to be known, in 1939, offering greater access to the team's blue-collar fans. A massive center-field scoreboard was installed in 1950, and was updated twice, along with the addition of box seats. Comiskey Park was also a venue for other events, including the 1937 boxing match in which Joe Louis became world heavyweight champion and the 1965 Chicago appearance of the Beatles. The Fab Four performed two shows on a plywood stage set up at second base while screaming fans were held back by police.

ABOVE: After the owner threatened to move the White Sox franchise, the city sought state financing to build a new facility on an adjacent lot. On September 30, 1990, the last game was played at the original Comiskey Park; America's oldest ballpark was torn down the following year. A plaque in the parking lot marks the old location of home plate, and the park is now named U.S. Cellular Field. The White Sox won the American League pennant in 2005 and went on to triumph in the World Series, their first title since 1917.

LEFT: Comiskey Park pictured in 1991 as U.S. Cellular Field rises next door.

c.1920

SEARS, ROEBUCK & CO. HEADQUARTERS / HOMAN SQUARE

From a time when Sears was the biggest mail-order company in the world

LEFT: Sears, Roebuck & Co. opened its headquarters in North Lawndale in 1906. Connected to downtown via the Burlington Railroad as well as a direct street route that would become Ogden Avenue, North Lawndale was a practical choice. Its new fireproof brick buildings were a lure for Chicago residents still reeling in the aftermath of the Great Fire. Already home to large industrial plants—including McCormick Reaper Works—North Lawndale materialized as an agreeable combination of Chicago's industrial and residential interests. The sprawling Sears complex covered more than forty-one acres, and contained 3 million square feet of office and factory space. It also housed the printing facility for the massive Sears catalog, and included its own power plant, water system, employee bank, and volunteer fire department. The company held social and athletic events at on-site facilities, which were converted to employee parking lots in 1926. The original fourteen-story Sears Tower (center) offered an observation deck for visitors. Sears, Roebuck & Co. relocated its headquarters to downtown's new 110-story Sears Tower in 1974.

BELOW: Once home to as much as a quarter of Chicago's Russian-Jewish population, North Lawndale's racial demographics began to shift in the 1950s. By 1960, the North Lawndale neighborhood was over 90 percent African American and heavily overcrowded. Residence and industry parted ways as former North Lawndale residents now commuted to work while much of the neighborhood's growing African American population remained unemployed. Racial tensions ran high, culminating in race riots following Martin Luther King Jr.'s assassination in 1968. Large employers began to relocate to areas that were more stable. Rising unemployment and the accompanying decline of the neighborhood drove many residents away, making North Lawndale one of Chicago's poorest neighborhoods. However, a unique partnership among Sears executives, city officials, developers, and community leaders brought about Homan Square, a project to revitalize North Lawndale in the early 1990s. Homan Square includes mixed-income housing, commercial space, and a community center. The 1906 tower—now Homan Square Tower—is listed on the National Register of Historic Places.

c.1927

LEFT: With the rise in automobile use among its employees, Sears converted the athletic facility to an employee parking lot in 1926.

c. 1929

CHINATOWN

The Chinese district of Chicago was created indirectly by a South Loop construction project

LEFT: Chicago's original Chinatown began in the 1870s with the arrival of Chinese workers on the vast system of railroads that all led to Chicago. The Midwest provided a more welcoming environment than the prohibitive sanctions meted out to Chinese people in the Western states. Settlement for Chinese in Chicago began around Clark and Van Buren Streets in the saloon-and-brothel-ridden First Ward, known as the Levee District. Vice gradually gave way to more legitimate business ventures downtown. The Chinese community moved farther south along Wentworth Avenue and Twenty-second Street. Modern Chinatown traces its origins to 1912, when a large group of Chinese immigrants was displaced from the South Loop by a construction project. The Chinese Benevolent Association negotiated fifty leases for shops and flats en masse, and Chinatown was born almost overnight.

ABOVE: After the revolution of Mao in China in the late 1940s, Chinese immigration to Chicago increased. A surge in population made the area more crowded, and Chinese immigrants took over a section of the community once the reserve of Italian and Croation immigrants in North Bridgeport. Two powerful urban development projects in the late 1950s and 1960s—the construction of the Dan Ryan Expressway and the Red Line elevated tracks—changed the contours of Chinatown. The area now flourishes more than ever. An expansion of commercial enterprise in the 1990s introduced a vast new center of shops, restaurants, and residential buildings. Chinatown's colorful lacquered gate is a symbol of the area's vibrancy and cultural enrichment. New immigrants, especially from Hong Kong, have brightened the commercial climate of this thriving neighborhood. Chinatown held a centennial parade in 2012 to celebrate 100 years of its South Side community.

LEFT: When Chicago architects Frost & Granger designed the Chicago Coliseum, they retained the battlements of the original structure—the rebuilt Libby Prison, which had been removed brick by brick from Richmond, Virginia, and relocated to 1513 South Wabash Avenue as a monument to the Union soldiers imprisoned there during the Civil War. This location south of the Loop allowed for a much larger public meeting space. When it opened in 1900, the Coliseum was the largest meeting space in the city, accommodating gatherings of up to 15,000 people. Its most popular attraction was the Chicago Auto Show, which was held at the Coliseum until 1935, when it moved to the International Amphitheatre at Forty-third and Halsted. The Coliseum was also home for the National Hockey League's Chicago Blackhawks from 1926 to 1929, when the team moved

ABOVE: The Coliseum continued to host many of Chicago's special events through the 1960s, including performances by Louis Armstrong as well as significant sporting events, such as the first professional basketball tournament played between African American and white teams in 1939. But 1971 was not a good year for the Coliseum. It was the site of a closed-circuit broadcast of the fight between Muhammad Ali and Joe Frazier, and when technical difficulties halted the broadcast in the third round, viewers rioted in protest. The building was cited for major violations to the city's fire code three days later. For the rest of the decade, the venue served mainly as storage space, and was finally demolished in 1982. The main structure on the site today is the Soka Gakkai Buddhist Center, which opened in 1995. Across the street, Coliseum Park honors the former arena

UNIVERSITY OF CHICAGO
The Ivy League of the Midwest

BELOW: In the early 1890s, oil baron John D. Rockefeller entered a partnership with Yale University professor William Rainey Harper to establish a university in the Midwest "to rival Princeton and Yale." On land donated by Marshall Field, Chicago architect Henry Ives Cobb designed the campus in a Gothic style resembling Oxford University. The University of Chicago opened in 1892 with an enrollment of 594 students. Architects Shepley, Rutan & Coolidge, designers of the Tower Group at Fifty-seventh Street and University Avenue, remained true to Cobb's original Gothic aesthetic, as did subsequent architects hired during the first half of the twentieth century. This complex includes the Mitchell Tower, named for John J. Mitchell, the wealthy Chicagoan who financed its construction.

c.1910

ABOVE: The Omlsted Brothers designed the Hull Coutyard and the gate in 1903.

ABOVE RIGHT: Walker Hall now borders the main quadrangle and houses the university's humanities division.

BELOW: Most universities gradually achieve renown over time, but the University of Chicago seemed to spring fully formed from the collaboration of its great early leaders. The school now has over 10,000 students attending prestigious graduate programs in law, medicine, business, and theology, among others. The school also claims sixty-seven Nobel Prize winners among its faculty and alumni, more than any other university.

1893

LEFT: Built on reclaimed swampland at the edge of the lakefront's Jackson Park, the "composite" building materials employed for the World's Columbian Exposition in 1893—a mixture of hemp and plaster—gave all its structures only a temporary life. However, after the fair's conclusion and a fire that destroyed most of the remaining buildings, this majestic structure, the former Palace of Fine Arts Building, became the first home of the Field Museum. In 1921 Julius Rosenwald, the president of Sears, Roebuck & Co., endowed a new museum. A $5 million renovation transformed the building into a more permanent Museum of Industry. In 1928 the name officially changed to the Museum of Science and Industry. Opening in 1933, it was ready for the second great Chicago World's Fair, the Century of Progress, celebrating the city's centennial.

ABOVE: After World War II, the Museum of Science and Industry became one of Chicago's most venerated attractions. Nothing captured people's attention more than the U-505, the German submarine captured on the high seas during the war. The man responsible for the capture, Captain (later Admiral) Daniel Gallery, was a Chicago native. He helped local business leaders acquire the U-boat from the U.S. Navy and have it brought through the St. Lawrence Seaway and all the Great Lakes to its new home. Once there, the submarine was lifted from the water and moved to a permanent home. In 2005 the vessel was moved to a special controlled exhibition site that protects this reminder of the last great global conflict. The museum today counts more than 350,000 square feet of space and welcomes over 2 million visitors each year.

c.1905

ABOVE: Frederick Law Olmsted designed Washington Park in 1871 as the "Upper Division" of great South Park, connected to the "Lower Division," or Jackson Park, via the narrow Midway Plaisance. Omsted's plans were destroyed by the Great Chicago Fire of 1871, and with the financial losses brought about by the disaster, new designer Horace W. S. Cleveland had to scale back Omsted's vision. The Washington Park Conservatory at Fifty-seventh Street and Cottage Grove Avenue, shown here in the early 1900s, was designed by Daniel Burnham in 1897. Most of the city parks' conservatories—including this one—were torn down during the Great Depression due to a lack of resources to maintain them.

WASHINGTON PARK

Part of the history of the "White City"

1889

ABOVE: This photo reveals the preference at the time for orderly garden designs.

BELOW: Neighborhood students christen a jeep at a June 1942 rally after purchasing more than $260,000 in war bonds.

1942

ABOVE: The park today resembles Olmsted's original vision to combine the best of nature and design. The northern end, 100 acres in all, comprises a large meadow, and the southern half includes a man-made lagoon with verdant landscaping. The park's vast acreage was proposed as the site of an Olympic stadium in Chicago's unsuccessful bid to host the 2012 Olympics. Today, the park is home to one of the best aquatic facilities in the city, as well as the DuSable Museum of African American History.

c.1960

RIVERVIEW PARK
Chicago's version of Coney Island

ABOVE: During the first decade of the 1900s, Chicago had more amusement parks than any city in the nation. Riverview Park opened in 1904 at Belmont and Western, and the front gate on Western Avenue was added two years later. Early attractions at the park included the River Walk, a five-row carousel, and the Battle of the *Monitor* and *Merrimac*, a re-creation of the famous naval battle of the Civil War. During the 1920s, Riverview Park had as many as eleven roller coasters in operation. One of these was the Bobs, which was built out of more than 3,200 feet of wooden track, including twelve curves and sixteen hills. Chicago building codes restricted the height of roller coaster hills, but builders often thwarted this law by digging trenches to extend the length of the drops.

1941

ABOVE: Visitors to Riverview Park celebrate German Day in 1941. German bands played and German beer flowed.

RIGHT: Riverview Park thrived throughout the 1950s and mid-1960s, adding new attractions and updating old ones each year, including a two-year restoration of the 1908 carousel. The park reopened in 1967, but at the end of that season, employees were informed that Riverview would be closing. Land values for the site had been rising, and offers from developers were becoming more frequent. Meanwhile, park revenues had been declining due to rising labor and maintenance costs. Real-estate developer Edgar F. Grimm purchased the land for $6 million—and reportedly received death threats from disappointed park goers in the process. Within a week, Grimm turned around his investment and the site was immediately cleared for development. The Chicago Police Department headquarters was one of the first buildings to go up, followed by the Riverview Plaza shopping mall (renamed Roscoe Plaza in 2011) and the DeVry Institute of Technology. The 1907 River Walk along the east bank is now overgrown with foliage.

RIGHT: This picture postcard from the early 1960s reveals the rows of electric lightbulbs that transformed the park's entrance into a magical gateway at night.

c. 1960

RIVERVIEW PARK

c. 1895

PULLMAN VILLAGE
A self-contained town within a city

ABOVE: Railroad magnate George M. Pullman established the Pullman Palace Car Company in 1867. In need of property for a new factory, Pullman purchased 4,000 acres of land on Chicago's far South Side. Rather than building a factory amid workers in the city, Pullman decided to build a city around his factory. Designed by prominent Chicago architect Solon Beman, who eventually designed a monument for Pullman's grave, the town of Pullman took a place among other American cities designed around an industry. Pullman employees and their families had everything they might need in the town of Pullman—schools, a library, a theater, a church, a bank, and a post office. All 20,000 of Pullman's workers were required to live in the community. This was an attractive option for Chicago's working-class families, who enjoyed tidy brick row houses with expensive modern conveniences for reasonable rents.

BELOW: Although many of the row house facades were identical, some sections included a variety of designs.

c.1895

ABOVE: Business plummeted during the Panic of 1893, so Pullman laid off thousands of workers and sliced wages 25 percent for those who remained. However, he refused to lower rents, resulting in near-starvation conditions. The workers went on strike, and in the spring of 1894 the American Railway Union, led by Eugene V. Debs, voted to support the Pullman strike. After a few episodes of violence, President Grover Cleveland sent in federal troops to break up the strike. Pullman died in 1897, and the town was sold to its residents in 1907. The entire district was declared a National Historic Landmark in 1971, but its isolated position ten miles from downtown Chicago has made a complete renaissance difficult.

1926

FRANK LLOYD WRIGHT HOME

"Study nature, love nature, stay close to nature. It will never fail you." —*Frank Lloyd Wright*

ABOVE: The original Frank Lloyd Wright home and studio, shown here in 1926, is at 951 Chicago Avenue in Oak Park, a suburb adjacent to the West Side. Wright's passion was residential design; in his career, he created over 270 homes, but this was his first. An apprentice in the office of Louis Sullivan, Wright was attracted to the Prairie style, and his designs ultimately came to define Prairie architecture. The style was heavily rooted in a Midwestern aesthetic—the use of natural building materials and a blending of residential space into its landscape to create a new, organic whole. By 1889, when he made this house his main residence, Wright had designed more than fifty Prairie-style homes, including the Robie House in Hyde Park and the distinctive Unity Temple in Oak Park. Wright used this house as a laboratory, constantly revising, rebuilding, and adding on. Wright lived here from 1889 to 1909 with his first wife, Catherine, and their six children.

BELOW: The original stone engraving still identifies the building's first owner.

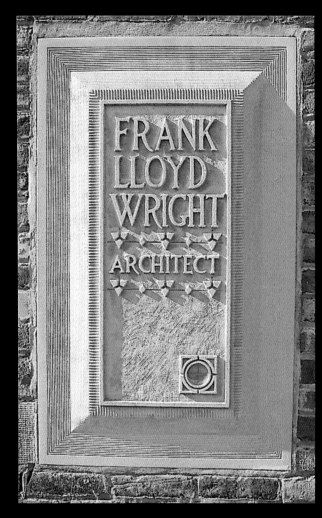

ABOVE: The house is now a National Historic Landmark and museum. The Frank Lloyd Wright Home and Studio Foundation has restored it to its 1909 appearance. The interior is also fully restored and features Art Deco wall paintings and a chain-supported balcony in the architecture studio. Oak Park boasts the world's largest collection of Wright-designed buildings. Wright lived in the suburb until 1909, when he left for Europe with his lover, Mamah Borthwick Cheney.